# Contents

## Introduction
Examinable skills .......................................................................... 4
Data-response skills ...................................................................... 5
Essay question skills...................................................................... 6
The synoptic requirement of the Unit 5 examination ............................. 7
Checklist of relevant Unit 1 terms.................................................... 7
A suggested strategy for tackling the examination................................ 8
Revision planning ......................................................................... 9

## Content Guidance
About this section........................................................................ 12
Introduction to the specification ..................................................... 13
Firms, production and costs............................................................ 15
Market structure and sales revenue.................................................. 20
Perfect competition and monopoly ................................................... 25
Oligopoly .................................................................................. 29
Evaluating market structures ......................................................... 34
Industrial policy .......................................................................... 40
Market failure and government failure .............................................. 45
The labour market ....................................................................... 52
Income, wealth and poverty........................................................... 58

## Questions and Answers
About this section........................................................................ 66
### Data-response questions
**Q1** The computer games market.................................................. 67
**Q2** Budget or low-cost airlines .................................................. 72
**Q3** Men and women in the labour market ...................................... 77
**Q4** Social security benefits and poverty in the UK ........................... 82

### Essay questions
**Q1** Objectives and growth of firms ............................................. 87
**Q2** Perfect competition ........................................................... 91
**Q3** Monopoly and economic efficiency.......................................... 94
**Q4** Market failure and government failure ..................................... 96
**Q5** Trade unions and the labour market........................................ 99

# Introduction

The aim of this guide is to prepare students for the AQA Advanced Level Unit 5 examination assessing A2 Module 5: Business Economics and the Distribution of Income. You should use the guide as follows:

**(1)** Read the introduction.

**(2)** The second and third sections of the book should then be used as supplements to other resources, such as class notes, textbooks, *Economic Review* magazine and *AS/A-Level Economics Revision Notes*. (The last two of these are published by Philip Allan Updates.) Because it contains summaries rather than in-depth coverage of all the topics in the specification, you should not use the guide as your sole learning resource during the main part of the course. However, you may well decide to use the guide as the main resource in your revision programme. You are strongly advised to make full use of the Questions and Answers section, especially in the revision period when you should be concentrating on improving your examination skills.

## Examinable skills

The Unit examination is 1½ hours long, has a maximum mark of 100 and contains two sections, **Section A** and **Section B**, which each count for 50 marks. There is **one** compulsory data-response question (DRQ) in Section A, and **three** essay questions (EQs) in Section B, of which you should answer **one. There are no multiple-choice questions in any of the three A2 Unit examination papers.**

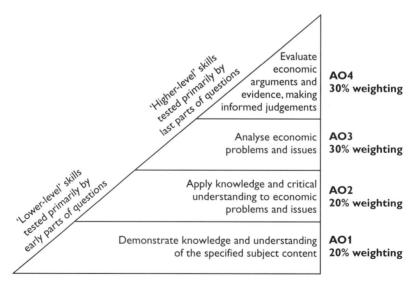

***Figure 1 The examination's assessment objectives arranged along the incline of difficulty***

The examination has four **assessment objectives** (AOs), shown in Figure 1 together with their examination weightings, arranged in an incline of difficulty. Lower-level skills of knowledge and **factual-recall** are shown in AO1 at the bottom of the incline. Moving up the incline, increasingly 'higher-level' skills feature in the AOs: **application of knowledge** and **critical understanding** (AO2); **analysis of problems** (AO3); and **evaluation of arguments and evidence** (AO4). Overall, 40% of the examination questions are knowledge-based, testing the lower-level skills in AOs 1 and 2. The remaining 60% of examination questions meet AOs 3 and 4. (In the AS examination, by contrast, 60% of the marks are awarded for lower-level skills and only 40% for higher-level skills. This means the A2 Unit examinations are more difficult than the AS Unit exams.)

## Data-response skills

The **compulsory data-response question** in Section A contains **four** sub-questions, listed as (a), (b), (c) and (d). The mark allocation is as follows: **part (a): 4 marks; part (b): 6 marks; part (c): 10 marks; and part (d): 30 marks**. The Unit 5 examination data-response question contains rather more data than AS data-response questions in the Unit 1 and 2 examinations. The layout and structure of the question will be similar to the five data-response questions in the Questions and Answers section of this guide. Each question is likely to contain two or three sets of data, usually extracted from different original sources, such as newspaper or magazine articles, or an internet website. The source will usually be indicated. With three data sets, the data will be labelled **Extract A, Extract B and Extract C**. One set of data is likely to be numerical, for example a line graph, a bar graph, a pie graph or a table. The other data set(s) will be text.

An 'incline of difficulty' will be built into the DRQ, with the earlier parts of the question being the most straightforward. Typically, the key instruction words for each part of the DRQ will be:

**(a) Describe** (or possibly **Compare**)

**(b) Explain**

**(c) Analyse**

**(d) Evaluate** (or possibly **Assess** or **Do you agree...?**, together with **Justify your argument**)

Parts (a) and (b) of the question will be marked using an **issue-based mark scheme** which lists the marks that can be awarded for the particular issues (and associated development) that might be included in the answer. Only lower-level skills (meeting AOs 1 and 2) are tested in parts (a) and (b) of the question.

As the key words indicate, parts (c) and (d) of the DRQ test the higher-level skills of **analysis** and **evaluation**. These parts of the question are marked using a **levels of response mark scheme**. The 'levels' mark scheme for part (c) of the DRQ has only **three levels, the content of which varies in every examination**.

Part (d) of the DRQ differs from the earlier parts (especially parts (a) and (b)) in three significant ways. First, and most obviously, the last part of the question carries many more marks than the earlier three parts — 60% of the total marks for the question and 30% of the total marks for the whole paper. If you time the examination incorrectly and fail to develop your answer to part (d) beyond a cursory footnote, you will reduce considerably your chance of achieving grade A. Second, whereas parts (a) and (b) should be answered briefly, you are expected to write an extended answer of least a page for part (d). Think of this as a 'mini' essay. (Part (c), which carries 10 marks, falls between these extremes. Its answer requires some development, but not as much as part (d).) Third, 'higher-level' skills of **analysis** and particularly **evaluation** are expected for part (d).

A levels of response mark scheme containing **five levels** is used for part (d) of the DRQ and for part (b) of all the essay questions in Section B. You must familiarise yourself with the 'levels' mark scheme and bear it in mind when you practice the last part of data-response questions and essay questions.

The key command word to **evaluate** or **assess** must be obeyed for your answer to reach the higher Level 4 and Level 5 standards of attainment set out in the levels of response mark scheme. Part (d) of the DRQ in Section A and part (b) of the essay questions in Section B are virtually the only parts of the whole examination paper set specifically to meet AO4: evaluation of arguments and evidence, and the making of informed judgements. (One mark out of ten in part (c) of the DRQ is also awarded for evaluation.) Your answer must evaluate the different arguments you set out. With many questions, discussion should centre on evaluating the advantages and disadvantages of (or the 'case for' versus the 'case against', or the costs and benefits of) a course of action mentioned in the question.

Finally, always try to finish your answer with a conclusion, the nature of which should vary according to the type of discussion or evaluation required. The conclusion might judge the relative strengths of the arguments discussed, possibly highlighting the most important argument. With many questions it is more appropriate to conclude whether, on balance, the 'case for' is stronger than the 'case against' and to provide some credible and reasoned justification for your opinion.

## Essay question skills

Whereas the DRQ in Section A of the Unit 5 examination is compulsory, you must select **one essay question from a choice of three** when answering Section B of the paper. Choice of question is obviously very important. As the questions in the Questions and Answers section of this book indicate, knowledge and understanding of imperfectly competitive and oligopolistic or highly concentrated markets will often be tested by the data-response question rather than by an essay question. But, because **business economics** accounts for approximately half the specification content, you should expect at least one essay question on the theory of the firm or a related topic. Related topics include: the market structures of perfect competition and monopoly, production and cost theory, how and why firms grow, and government competition policy.

You should also expect one essay question on the labour market, and/or distributions of income and/or wealth and/or poverty, and one question on another area of the specification, such as market failure and/or government failure, cost–benefit analysis, etc.

The key instruction words for the two parts of each essay question are likely to be:
**(a) Explain**
**(b) Evaluate** (or possibly **Assess** or **Do you agree...?**, together with **Justify your argument**)

As is the case with parts (a) and (b) of the data-response question, part (a) of the essay question tests the lower-level skills and assessment objectives of knowledge and understanding, and application. The advice already given on how to answer part (d) of the compulsory data-response question is equally applicable to answering part (b) of your chosen essay question.

## The synoptic requirement of the Unit 5 examination

It is important to realise that the Unit 5 and Unit 6 examinations at A-level are **synoptic**. To understand what this means, you should compare the Unit 5 examination with the Unit 1 AS examination on Markets and Market Failure. Questions in the Unit 1 examination must only test knowledge and understanding of terms and concepts set out in the AQA Module 1 specification. For example, a Unit 1 examination cannot contain a question on a market which requires the candidate to apply a macroeconomic concept (for example, the influence of the business cycle) to explain a shift of the demand curve in the market. Booms and recessions are in the Module 2: National Economy specification and not in the Module 1 specification.

A question such as this could, however, appear in the Unit 5 examination. It illustrates both vertical synopticity and horizontal synopticity. **Horizontal synopticity** requires the application of a Module 6 macroeconomic concept or theory to answer a Unit 5 microeconomic question. By contrast, **vertical synopticity** requires the use of AS microeconomic concepts and theories (in the Module 1 specification) to answer Unit 5 microeconomic questions. It is important to note the following points:
**(1)** There is no mention of supply and demand (except in the context of the labour market) in the Module 5 specification, yet it is vital that you remember and revise this extremely important element of microeconomics, including elasticity.
**(2)** Market failures such as public goods, externalities, merit and demerit goods are not mentioned explicitly in the Module 5 specification, but you may be required in the Unit 5 examination to develop and extend material learnt for AS, particularly in relation to resource allocation and misallocation.

## Checklist of relevant Unit 1 terms

Here is a checklist of Unit 1 AS terms, concepts and theories, not mentioned in the Module 5 specification, which might be needed for the Unit 5 exam:
- the purpose of economic activity
- the economic problem, scarcity, the need for choice and opportunity cost
- economic resources and factors of production

- the nature of a competitive market
- supply and demand diagrams, equilibrium, disequilibrium, excess demand, excess supply
- shifts of demand and supply curves
- elasticity: price elasticity of demand and supply, income elasticity of demand, cross elasticity of demand
- substitutes, complementary goods and derived demand
- normal goods and inferior goods
- how changes in one market can affect other markets
- the signalling, incentive and rationing (allocative) functions of prices
- causes of market failure: public goods, positive and negative externalities, merit goods, demerit goods
- government policies to make markets work better and to correct market failure: taxation, subsidy, redistribution, regulation, tradable permits to pollute, price controls, buffer stock policies
- government failure

## A suggested strategy for tackling the examination

**(1)** On opening the examination booklet, turn to Section B and spend a minute or so reading all three essay questions before making a preliminary choice of a favoured question. For each question, look carefully at part (b), which is the part for which higher-level analysis and evaluation marks are awarded. Beware of choosing a question with an apparently straightforward part (a), but a part (b) that you do not fully understand.

**(2)** Then go back to Section A, glance through the questions at the end of the data, and then spend about 3 minutes reading the extracts containing the data.

**(3)** Assuming you have 40 minutes to answer the data-response question, write the following time allocations in the margin against each part of the question: part (a) 3 minutes; part (b) 5 minutes; part (c) 8 minutes; part (d) 24 minutes.

**(4)** Answer all the parts of the question, preferably in the correct order, sticking rigidly to the time allocation. Do not over-develop your answers to parts (a) and (b) of the question, but remember that a single-sentence answer seldom answers the question properly. Remember also that many candidates fail to do themselves justice in the exam because they overwrite their answers to parts (a) and (b), and do not leave enough time to answer part (d) properly.

**(5)** Clearly label each answer with the correct letter: (a), (b), (c), (d). Nothing annoys an examiner more than a script in which all the answers are jumbled together.

**(6)** Do not waste time copying out the questions, but leave a few lines at the end of each part of your answer in case you have time at the end of the exam to add an extra sentence or two.

**(7)** For each part of the question, think very carefully about what it requires you to do, and make sure you **obey** the key instruction word.

**(8)** You probably will not have time to write plans for each part of the question, except part (d), where a short plan might help you to write a better answer.

**(9)** Having completed your answer to the compulsory data-response question in Section A, turn the page to Section B, and read the questions carefully again. Choose the question that you think you can answer best, taking into account the difficulty of *both* parts of the question.

**(10)** Assuming you have 45 minutes to answer your chosen question, write the following time allocations in the margin against each part of the question: part (a) 18 minutes; part (b) 27 minutes. This time allocation, which uses up all the available time, can be shortened slightly to allow yourself up to 5 minutes to read through all your answers to *both* the data-response question and the essay question when you have completed both parts of the essay question.

**(11)** If you believe it will help you, write a short plan for part (a). Then write your answer to part (a), making sure you define all terms and concepts you apply — both those in the wording of the question and those you introduce from your own knowledge. You need to display the skills of **knowledge and understanding, application**, and perhaps some **analysis**, to stand a chance of gaining full marks for part (a) of the essay question.

**(12)** Having completed your answer to part (a) within 18 minutes, write a plan for part (b). If appropriate, list the 'case for' and the 'case against' arguments you intend to develop in your answer. Also, list any theories you are going to use to analyse the issue(s) posed by the question.

**(13)** Start your answer to part (b) by stating how you are interpreting the question, and by indicating briefly the arguments to be developed in the main body of your answer. Then develop each argument, making sure you use appropriate theory and analysis. You can also pick up evaluation marks if you indicate, as you go along, how significant each argument is. But make sure you write a concluding paragraph, several lines long, devoted to an overview of the arguments and containing an overall conclusion. This is where the examiner finds it easiest to award evaluation marks.

(The advice given in points (12) and (13) above is equally applicable for answering part (d) of the compulsory data-response question in Section A of the examination.)

## Revision planning

The revision strategy below is based on the use of this guide, supplemented by other resources such as the notes you have built up over your course of study and favoured textbooks. The programme is designed for the 3-week period before the examination. The strategy assumes you are revising at least two other A-level subjects (and for the Unit 6: Government Policy, the National and International Economy examination) during the same period, but are able to devote a session of 2 hours (plus half an hour for short breaks) to Unit 5 every other day, with shorter follow-up sessions on the intervening days. You should revise solidly for 6 days a week, but allow yourself one day off a week to recharge your batteries. The strategy can be modified to meet your personal needs and preferences: for example, by shortening each revision session and/or extending the sessions over a revision period longer than 3 weeks.

**(1)** Revise one topic from the Content Guidance section of this guide per revision session. Divide the revision session into four half-hour periods during which you are working solidly and without distraction, interspersed with 10-minute breaks.

**(2)** Proceed through the topics in the order they appear in the guide:

Week 1: Topics 1–3

Week 2: Topics 4–6

Week 3: Topics 7–9

**(3)** Vary the activities you undertake in each 30-minute period of a revision session. For example, spend the first 30 minutes reading through the Essential Information section of the topic. List key terms and concepts on a piece of paper. After a short break, use the second 30-minute period to check more fully the meaning of the key terms and concepts in your class notes and/or an economics textbook. Then after a second short break, check which essay questions and parts of data-response questions in the Questions and Answers section of the guide test aspects of the topic you are revising. Spend the rest of the 30 minutes answering some or all of the questions. In the final 30-minute period — or perhaps in a follow-up session a day or two later — carefully read through any candidate answers that relate to the parts of the essay question or DRQ covered by the topic, and also read the examiner's comments on the question(s).

To vary your revision programme, and to make sure you reinforce and retain the vital information revised in the longer sessions, you should fit some of the activities suggested below into follow-up sessions. Activities suitable for follow-up and 10-minute sessions include the following:

- **Write definitions** of some key terms and concepts relating to the topic revised on the previous day. Check each of your definitions against the correct definition in this guide, or in a textbook or your class notes.
- **Draw key diagrams** relating to the topic. Check any diagram you draw against a correct version of the diagram, making absolutely sure that the diagram is correctly and clearly labelled.
- Whenever you make mistakes, **repeat these exercises** every day or so, until you have eliminated all the mistakes.
- **Answer questions** from past AQA examination papers and from AQA's *Specimen Units and Mark Schemes* booklet, which your teacher should have. Make sure your teacher obtains all the relevant June and January AQA past exam papers that are available at the time you take the examination. Identify and then answer questions from past papers, which relate to the topic just revised. Then spend another follow-up session checking your answer(s) against the AQA mark scheme(s) to see how you could improve your answer(s).

**Note:** if you wish to buy your own copies of past examination papers and mark schemes, contact: The Publications Department, The Assessment and Qualifications Alliance, Aldon House, 39 Heald Grove, Manchester M14 4NA (tel: 0161 953 1170).

# Content
# Guidance

In contrast to AS Module 1: Markets and Market Failure, which is concerned with **elementary** microeconomics, Module 5: Business Economics and the Distribution of Income centres for the most part on more **advanced** microeconomics. As the specification states, Module 5 builds on the knowledge and skills learnt in Module 1. It requires candidates to use and evaluate more complex microeconomic models — for example, perfect competition, monopoly and oligopoly — and to develop further a critical approach to such economic models and methods of enquiry.

In this module, examination candidates are required to develop a more formal understanding of economic efficiency and the arguments for and against government intervention in markets than is required at AS. You will also be expected to apply your knowledge and skills in a wider range of contexts than required in Module 1, and to propose solutions to problems. These additional contexts include education and training, and utility markets such as electricity, gas, water and telecommunications.

Unlike in Module 1, the labour market is an important part of Module 5. The module also includes a number of topics that are linked to the macroeconomic content of Module 6: Government Policy, the National and International Economy. These are: the distribution of income and wealth, the causes of poverty, and the use of the fiscal policy instruments of taxation and public spending to reduce poverty and income inequalities.

The introduction to this section of the guide (pp. 13–14) contains a summary of the AQA specification for Module 5: Business Economics and the Distribution of Income. This is followed by more detail about each section of the specification under the following headings:
- Firms, production and costs (pp. 15–20)
- Market structure and sales revenue (pp. 20–24)
- Perfect competition and monopoly (pp. 25–29)
- Oligopoly (pp. 29–34)
- Evaluating market structures (pp. 34–39)
- Industrial policy (pp. 40–45)
- Market failure and government failure (pp. 45–51)
- The labour market (pp. 52–58)
- Income, wealth and poverty (pp. 58–64)

# Introduction to the specification

The AQA specification for Unit 5 contains the following sections.

## 14.1 Theory of the firm

This specification section covers knowledge of **short-run** and **long-run production** (including the **law of diminishing returns** and **returns to scale**), knowledge of how **cost curves** are derived from production theory in both the short run and the long run, and an understanding of **economies of scale** and **diseconomies of scale** in relation to a firm's **long-run average cost curve**. The concepts of **fixed cost** and **variable cost**, and **marginal cost**, **short-run average cost** and **total cost** must also be understood, along with **total, average** and **marginal revenue**. Knowledge of **profit**, which is the difference between revenue and cost, is required, and candidates must be familiar with the concepts of **normal** and **abnormal** (or **supernormal**) **profit.** You must understand the profit-maximising objective of firms, together with **alternative objectives to profit maximisation** such as **satisficing**. You must also understand the reason for the separation or **divorce of ownership from control** in modern industrial economies and how this affects the conduct and performance of firms.

## 14.2 Competitive markets

This section of the Module 5 specification introduces the economist's model of **perfect competition**. You must know how, subject to certain assumptions, perfect competition results in **efficient resource allocation**, and how consumers benefit from competitive markets. You must be able to handle a **formal diagrammatic analysis of perfect competition**, in the **short run** and the **long run**, and at the level of both the **whole market** and a **single firm within the market**.

## 14.3 Concentrated markets

This section of the specification covers two important **market structures** in the real economy: **monopoly** and **oligopoly**, where firms are **price-makers** rather than **price-takers**. You must know how to evaluate and compare the **conduct** (or **behaviour**) and **performance** of firms within these market structures with the conduct and performance of perfectly competitive firms. You may be asked to apply **efficiency concepts** to analyse and evaluate the **performance** and **desirable and less desirable characteristics** of monopoly, oligopoly and perfect competition. You must also analyse market structures in terms of gains, losses and transfers of **economic welfare**, in the form of **consumer surplus** and **producer surplus**. You must understand how **uncertainty** and **interdependence**, in both **competitive oligopoly** and **collusive oligopoly** (for example, in **cartels**), affect firms' behaviour, leading to different forms of **price setting**, including **price discrimination**. The role of **entry barriers** in protecting monopoly power is also important. You must appreciate how **market contestability** affects industry performance, and the roles of **sunk costs** and **hit and run competition**.

## 14.4 The labour market

This section of the specification requires application of **supply and demand theory** to the economy's **labour markets**. You must understand how the **demand for labour** is a **derived demand**, explained in part by **marginal productivity theory** and the **law of diminishing returns** (in specification section 14.1). It is important to distinguish between demand for, and supply of, labour in the *whole* of a labour market, and at the level of a *particular firm* (or employer) and an *individual worker* within the labour market.

In **perfectly competitive labour markets**, individual firms and workers are passive **price-takers** at the ruling market wage set in the market as a whole. By contrast, in **monopsony** labour markets, a single employer or buyer of labour has the market power to set the wage rate below the value of the marginal product of labour. Monopsony employers can also engage in **wage discrimination**, and **discrimination according to gender, race or religion**. You must understand the various factors that affect the **ability of trade unions to influence wages**, and analyse the effect on employment of a **union setting a wage above the free-market wage**, both in a perfectly competitive labour market and in monopsony. Knowledge of the **distribution of income and wealth** in the UK is expected, and of the **factors influencing the distribution**.

## 14.5 Government intervention in the market

The specification requires application of **efficiency and welfare criteria**, particularly **allocative efficiency and inefficiency**, to explain and analyse market failures and related policy solutions. The use of **marginalist analysis** is expected, particularly the use of diagrams showing **marginal private cost and benefit** and **marginal social cost and benefit**. Market failures associated with **environmental change** are likely to figure in examination questions. Explanation, analysis and evaluation of government policies to correct market failure is expected. This may centre on policies currently used, such as **taxation** and **regulation**, and policies yet to be introduced (in the UK), such as establishing markets in **permits to pollute** and in **property rights**. You must appreciate how government intervention to correct or reduce market failure may create new problems of **government failure** such as **regulatory capture**, which occurs when regulators, who are meant to protect the interests of consumers, side instead with the producers they are supposed to regulate. When assessing the costs and benefits of government intervention, you must understand the principles of **cost–benefit analysis (CBA)** and be able to evaluate the advantages and disadvantages of using CBA. Two topics in this specification section, **competition policy** and **poverty**, link to topics encountered earlier in the module specification. Competition policy tries to make goods markets (or product markets) more competitive and efficient. **Government policies to reduce poverty** aim to make the distribution of income and wealth less unequal. When evaluating the success of these policies, you must understand the difference between **absolute poverty** and **relative poverty**, and the difference between **vertical and horizontal equity**.

# Firms, production and costs

These notes, which relate to AQA specification sections 14.1 and 14.2, prepare you to answer AQA examination questions on:

- firms and their objectives
- production theory
- costs of production

## Essential information

### Firms and their objectives

There are many different types of **business** or **firm**, ranging from very small one-person businesses, performing functions such as painting and decorating, to massive companies such as British Petroleum (BP), at the opposite end of the size spectrum. The latter are often **multinational firms** owning and controlling subsidiary companies and establishments throughout the world. In most instances, the largest companies are also **multi-product** firms, producing and selling different goods and services in a number of different markets.

Economists usually assume that firms have a single business objective: to **maximise profit**. However, real-world firms may have other objectives: to **maximise sales revenue**; to **maximise the growth of the business**; or to **maximise managerial objectives**. The last is significant when there is a **divorce of ownership from control** in a business, which occurs in large firms organised as **public limited companies (plcs)**. Plcs are owned by thousands of shareholders who employ managers or executives to run the business. As recent business scandals in firms such as Enron and Worldcom have shown, the managers may pursue their own agendas, maximising their own pay etc. and making decisions that are not in the interest of the owners of the business.

So far we have assumed that firms have a maximising objective, be it profit, sales revenue, growth, or management pay and creature comforts. However, some firms may be best modelled as **satisficers** rather than *maximisers*. Under this assumption, decision makers in firms, be they the owners of small corner shops or the chief executives of huge plcs, may be content with a **satisfactory outcome**, say satisfactory profit, rather than the best possible outcome. They may be happy with an easy life.

### Production

Firms produce goods or services for sale at a price in markets. **Production** converts **inputs** into **outputs** of useful goods and services. The *inputs* necessary for production to take place, which include the services of **labour, capital** and **land**, are known as the **factors of production**. Economists also identify a fourth factor of production, **enterprise** or the entrepreneurial input. The **entrepreneur** is the financial risk taker and decision maker. In a small business, the owner combines both these functions, bearing the financial risks, but also reaping the financial rewards, and deciding such questions as **what**, **how** and **how much to produce**. However, with the divorce between ownership and control in many large firms, the **entrepreneurial function is split** between owners (shareholders) and the salaried managers they employ.

### The short run and the long run

The **short run** is the period of time in which **at least one factor of production is fixed**. In the short run, a firm can increase output or supply only by adding more of a variable factor, such as labour, to the fixed factors of production such as capital and land. Also, firms cannot enter or leave a market in the short run. In the **long run, all the factors of production are variable** and a firm can increase output or supply by changing the *scale* of the factors held fixed in the short run. Only in the long run can a firm either expand the scale of its operations by increasing capacity, or reduce its activities by closing down plant. The long run is also the time period in which new firms can enter a market or industry and existing firms can leave, providing no barriers exist to prevent freedom of entry and exit.

### Short-run production and the law of diminishing returns

Suppose a small manufacturing firm decides to employ only one worker. The worker must be a 'jack-of-all-trades', doing all tasks involved in production. But if more workers are hired, output can rise at a faster rate than the number of workers employed. This is because the workers benefit from **specialisation** and the **division of labour**, as production tasks are divided between the workers. In this situation, the **marginal product** of labour increases. Marginal product (or **marginal returns**) is the increase in output that results from adding an extra worker to the labour force.

But eventually, as more and more workers are combined with the firm's fixed capital, the benefits of further specialisation and division of labour come to an end. The **law of diminishing returns** (also known as the **law of diminishing marginal productivity**) sets in when the marginal product of labour starts to fall: that is, when one more worker adds less to total output than the previous worker who joined the labour force.

### Long-run production and returns to scale

The law of diminishing returns is a **short-run law** which does not operate in the **long run**, when a firm can increase the **scale** of all its inputs or factors of production. You must not confuse the short-run law of diminishing returns with **returns to scale** which occur only in the long run. With returns to scale there are three possibilities:

- **Increasing returns to scale:** an increase in the scale of all the factors of production causes a more than proportionate increase in output.
- **Decreasing returns to scale:** an increase in the scale of all the factors of production causes a less than proportionate increase in output.
- **Constant returns to scale:** an increase in the scale of all the factors of production causes an exactly proportionate increase in output.

### Short-run costs

In the short run, a firm's **total costs of production** divide into **fixed costs** (the cost of employing the fixed factors of production, such as capital) and **variable costs** (the cost of employing the variable factors of production, such as labour). **Total fixed costs (TFC)**, or **overheads**, are shown by the constant or horizontal line in the left-hand panel of Figure 1. The right-hand panel shows **average fixed costs (AFC)**, which fall as overheads are spread over larger levels of output.

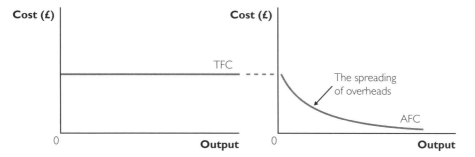

*Figure 1 Total fixed costs and average fixed costs*

Figure 2 shows an **average variable cost (AVC)** curve, with a **marginal cost (MC)** curve rising and cutting through the lowest point on the AVC curve. **Marginal cost is the extra cost of producing one more unit of output**. The shape of the MC curve is explained by marginal productivity theory. As long as the marginal productivity of labour is increasing, then, assuming all workers are paid the same wage rate, the cost of producing an extra unit of output falls. Hence marginal costs fall at low levels of output. But as soon as the law of diminishing returns sets in, each worker hired adds less to total output than the previous worker taken on. Total costs of production rise faster than output, leading to rising marginal costs.

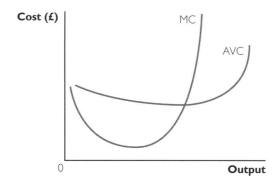

*Figure 2 Average variable costs (AVC) and marginal costs (MC)*

Figure 2 provides an illustration of the very important relationship between any marginal curve and the average curve plotted from the same data:

- when the marginal > the average, the average rises
- when the marginal < the average, the average falls
- when the marginal = the average, the average is constant, neither rising nor falling

The relationship between marginal and average curves has several economic applications: **marginal and average product curves** (in production theory); **marginal** and average cost curves (illustrated in Figures 2 and 3); and, as we shall see in the next topic, **marginal and average revenue curves**. You must understand this relationship. It does *not* state that an average curve will rise when the related marginal curve is rising, or that the average curve must fall when the related marginal curve falls. Study Figure 2 carefully. After diminishing returns set in, the **MC curve** starts to rise, *but* the **AVC curve** continues to fall as long as marginal costs are *below* average variable costs. Eventually, however, the MC curve rises through the AVC curve, causing the AVC curve also to rise. As a result, the AVC curve is U-shaped, with the MC curve cutting through the curve at its lowest point.

The left-hand panel of Figure 3 shows how the firm's **average total cost (ATC)** curve is obtained by adding up the AFC and AVC curves. The right-hand panel of Figure 3 shows the ATC curve without its two 'building blocks' (AFC and AVC). The ATC curve is U-shaped, showing that average total costs per unit of output first fall and later rise as output is increased. ATC must eventually rise because, at high levels of output, any further spreading of fixed costs is insufficient to offset the impact of diminishing returns upon variable costs of production. Eventually, rising marginal costs (which, as we have seen, result from diminishing marginal returns) must cut through and pull up the ATC curve.

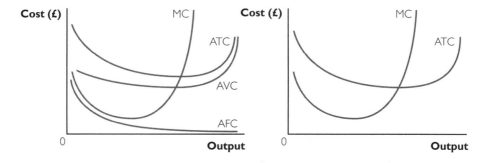

*Figure 3 The average total cost curve obtained by adding AVC to AFC*

### Long-run average costs, and economies and diseconomies of scale

Just as the short-run law of diminishing returns explains rising marginal costs and (eventually, when marginal costs cut through average total costs) rising average total costs, so we use long-run production theory concepts to explain the firm's **long-run average cost (LRAC)** curve, illustrated in Figure 4. If, as the firm increases the size or scale of all its factors of production, it benefits from increasing returns to scale, the LRAC curve will fall. Falling long-run average costs are known as **economies of scale**. Conversely, rising long-run average costs are known as **diseconomies of scale**. You should notice that a number of **short-run average total cost (SRATC) curves**, labelled $SRATC_1$, $SRATC_2$ and $SRATC_3$, have been drawn in Figure 4, and that the LRAC curve touches (or is tangential to) each SRATC curve. Each SRATC curve represents a particular short-run size or scale of firm.

The left-hand panel of Figure 4 shows a **U-shaped LRAC curve** in which economies of scale and falling long-run average costs give way beyond $SRATC_3$ to diseconomies of scale. $SRATC_3$ represents the **lowest unit cost** and most **productively efficient** size of firm. This is also called the **optimum size of firm**. However, other shapes of LRAC curve are also possible. The right-hand panel of Figure 4 shows an **L-shaped LRAC curve**. The size of firm represented by $SRATC_3$ in this diagram is called **minimum efficient scale (MES)**. It is sited at the point on the LRAC curve beyond which no more economies of scale are possible. But there are no diseconomies of scale, so all sizes of firms beyond MES are equally productively efficient.

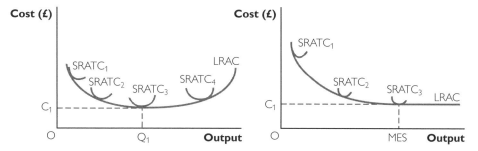

*Figure 4 Long-run average cost curves*

## Examination questions and skills

Essay question 1 (EQ1) tests knowledge and understanding of the objectives of firms, and aspects of the growth of firms. Part (a) of DRQ2 asks for a brief explanation of why two airlines incur different costs.

Examination questions which require detailed explanation of the shape and slope of cost curves are *not* likely to be set. Rather, questions will test your ability to select an appropriate cost curve diagram to use in the explanation, analysis and/or evaluation of, for example, the growth of firms, economies of scale, the nature of production, economic efficiency, and firms' conduct and performance in the different market structures of perfect competition, monopoly and oligopoly.

## Common examination errors

Commonly made mistakes on firms, production and costs include the following:
- Assuming that all firms have a single objective — profit maximisation.
- Confusing the short run and the long run, both for production theory and for cost curves.
- Using the long-run concept of economies of scale to explain short-run cost curves.
- Showing no understanding of the relationship between marginal and average costs.
- Badly drawn cost curves, incorrectly labelled with the MC curve in the wrong position.

- Confusing marginal and average returns with marginal and average revenue.
- Writing long irrelevant descriptive answers — for example, on types of economy of scale — when the question requires analysis and the application of theory rather than description.

# Market structure and sales revenue

These notes, which relate to AQA specification sections 14.1, 14.2 and 14.3, prepare you to answer AQA examination questions on:
- differences between the three market structures of perfect competition, monopoly and oligopoly
- revenue curves in perfect competition and monopoly
- the MR = MC rule and profit maximisation

## Essential information

### Market structures

Whereas cost curves derive from production theory and the cost of hiring the factors of production, a firm's **revenue curves** depend on the **market structure** in which it sells its output. Figure 5 shows the main structures recognised by economists.

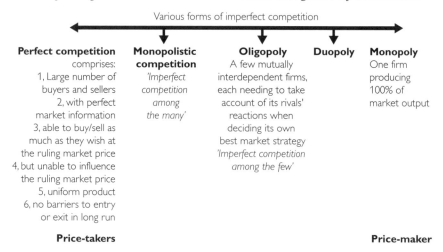

*Figure 5 The main market structures*

**Perfect competition** and **monopoly** are at opposite ends of the spectrum shown in Figure 5. In a perfectly competitive market there are a very large number of firms. By contrast in monopoly (or strictly **pure monopoly**), a single firm produces the whole of the output of a market or industry. A pure monopolist faces no competition at all, since there are no other firms to compete against. Monopolists do, however, usually face some competitive pressures, both from substitute products and sometimes also from outside firms trying to enter the market to destroy their monopoly position. Pure monopoly is exceedingly rare and often the word 'monopoly' is used in a looser sense to refer to any **highly concentrated market**, in which one firm is dominant.

Every market structure between the extremes of perfect competition and monopoly is a form of **imperfect competition**. There are two main forms of imperfect competition: oligopoly and monopolistic competition. An **oligopoly** is a market dominated by a few large interdependent firms. **Interdependence** means that an oligopolist has to take account of the likely reactions of the other firms when deciding price and output. **Duopoly** is a special case of oligopoly in which there are just two dominant firms. By contrast to oligopoly, which is sometimes called 'imperfect competition among the few', **monopolistic competition** is 'imperfect competition among the many'. However, monopolistic competition, in which a large number of firms produce goods slightly differentiated by fashion and style, is *not* a part of the AQA specification, so no further mention is made of monopolistic competition in this book.

Perfect competition is an abstract economic model that does not actually exist in any real-world market. This is because the conditions listed in Figure 5 which define perfect competition are too demanding and never occur together at once. Competitive markets in the real world are examples of imperfect competition rather than perfect competition, though some highly competitive markets such as commodity and financial markets possess some of the features of perfect competition.

**Revenue curves in perfect competition**
A perfectly competitive firm's revenue curves are derived from the assumptions, listed in Figure 5, that the firm can sell whatever quantity it wishes at the ruling market price, but that it cannot influence the ruling market price by its own action.

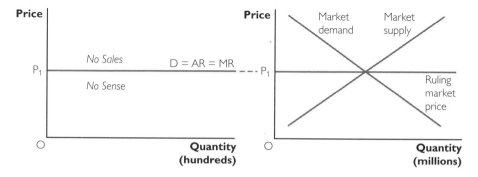

*Figure 6 Deriving the AR and MR curves of a perfectly competitive firm*

The right-hand panel of Figure 6 shows the whole of a perfectly competitive market, whereas the left-hand panel shows the situation facing a single firm within the market.

The ruling market price $P_1$ is determined in the right-hand panel, where market demand equals market supply. In the left-hand panel of the diagram, each firm faces an **infinitely elastic** (or **perfectly elastic**) demand curve located at $P_1$, the ruling price set by market forces in the whole market. Consider also the two slogans **no sales** and **no sense**, which are respectively above and below $P_1$. Suppose, first, that the firm tries to set a price above $P_1$. Possessing perfect market information, the firm's customers immediately stop buying, deciding instead to buy the identical products (which are perfect substitutes) available at $P_1$ which are produced by other firms in the market — hence 'no sales'. But if the firm can sell as much as it wishes at the ruling price, there is no point in reducing the price below $P_1$. No extra sales are gained, but the firm loses sales revenue (and profit) — hence 'no sense'. We conclude that a perfectly competitive firm is a **price-taker**, passively accepting but unable to influence the ruling market price.

As well as being the perfectly elastic demand curve for the firm's output, the horizontal line drawn through $P_1$ is also the perfectly competitive firm's **average revenue (AR) curve** and its **marginal revenue (MR) curve**. Every time it sells one more unit of output, total sales revenue rises by the price at which the extra unit is sold ($P_1$). Thus marginal revenue is $P_1$. And because revenue per unit sold is always the same however much is sold, average revenue is $P_1$ at all levels of output and sales.

### Monopoly revenue curves

Monopoly revenue curves differ from those facing a firm in a perfectly competitive market. Because there is only one firm in the market, the market demand curve is the demand curve for the monopolist's output. This means that the monopolist faces a downward-sloping demand curve, whose elasticity is determined by the nature of consumer demand for the monopolist's product. The demand curve can affect the monopolist in one of two different ways. If we regard the monopolist as a **price-maker**, then whenever it sets the price, the demand curve determines how much it can sell. If the monopolist tries to raise the price, it must accept a fall in sales. Alternatively, if the monopolist decides to act as a **quantity setter**, the demand curve dictates the maximum price at which any chosen quantity can be sold. Thus the downward-sloping demand curve means that the monopolist faces a trade-off. A monopoly cannot set price and quantity independently of each other.

Because the demand curve shows the price that the monopolist charges at each level of output, the **demand curve is the monopolist's average revenue curve**. Unlike perfect competition, however, marginal revenue and average revenue in monopoly are not the same. Because the average revenue curve falls, the marginal revenue curve must be below it. (If you don't understand this, check the explanation of average and marginal curves in the previous topic, p. 21.) This is illustrated in the left-hand panel of Figure 7. Note that the MR curve is twice as steep as the AR curve. This is always the case whenever the AR curve is both downward sloping and a straight line.

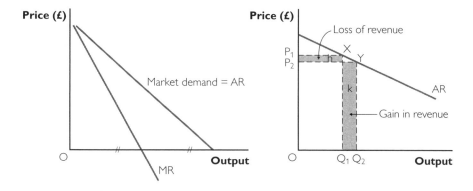

*Figure 7 Monopoly average revenue and marginal revenue curves*

The relationship between AR and MR in monopoly can also be explained in another way that is illustrated in the right-hand panel of Figure 7. Because the demand curve (or AR curve) is downward sloping, the monopolist can sell an extra unit of output only by reducing the price (and average revenue) of all units of output sold. In this situation, total sales revenue *increases* by the shaded area **k** on the diagram, but *decreases* by the shaded area **h**. Area **k** shows a **revenue gain**, namely the extra unit sold multiplied by its price. By contrast, area **h** shows a **revenue loss**. The revenue loss results from the fact that, in order to sell one more unit of output, the price has to be reduced for *all* units of output, not just the extra unit sold. Marginal revenue = the revenue gain *minus* the revenue loss, which must be less than price or average revenue.

### The MR = MC rule and profit maximisation

We noted in the previous topic that economists generally assume that firms have a single objective: **profit maximisation. Total profit = total revenue (TR) – total cost (TC)**, and a firm aims to produce the level of output at which TR – TC is maximised. However, it is often more convenient to state the condition required for profit maximisation as: **marginal revenue = marginal cost, or simply MR = MC**.

MR = MC means that a firm's profits are greatest when the addition to sales revenue received from the last unit sold (**marginal revenue**) equals exactly the addition to total cost incurred from the production of the last unit of output (**marginal cost**). Consider a farmer producing tomatoes for sale in a local market who is unable to influence the ruling market price of 50p per kilo. At any size of sales, average revenue is 50p, which also equals marginal revenue. Suppose that when the farmer markets 300 kilos of tomatoes, the cost of producing and marketing the 300th kilo is 48p. By deciding not to market the kilo, he sacrifices 2p of profit. Suppose now that total costs rise by 50p and 52p respectively when a 301st kilo and a 302nd kilo are marketed. The marketing of the 302nd kilo causes profits to fall by 2p, but the 301st kilo of tomatoes leaves total profits unchanged: it represents the level of sales at which profits are exactly maximised.

To sum up:
- when MR > MC, profits rise when output and sales increase
- and when MR < MC, profits rise when output and sales fall
- so only when MR = MC are profits maximised

It is important to realise that MR = MC is the condition for profit maximisation in all market structures. In perfect competition, monopoly and oligopoly, profit maximisation occurs only at the level of output and sales at which MR = MC.

## Examination questions and skills

Part (a) of EQ1 tests knowledge and understanding of the profit-maximising objective of firms, and requires illustration of the MR = MC rule on a diagram (see the next topic, 'Perfect competition and monopoly', pp. 25–29). Part (a) of EQ2 asks for an explanation of how price and output are determined in perfect competition. Revenue curves do not figure explicitly in any of the data-response questions in this book, but knowledge of market structure and awareness of the profit-maximising objective are relevant for DRQs 1 and 2.

As with cost curves, examination questions which require detailed explanation of the shape and slope of revenue curves are *not* likely to be set. Rather, questions will test your ability to select an appropriate revenue curve diagram to use (probably in conjunction with cost curves) to analyse a particular market structure: perfect competition, monopoly or oligopoly. How to do this is explained in the next four topics.

## Common examination errors

Commonly made mistakes on market structure and sales revenue include the following:
- Confusing marginal and average revenue curves with average and marginal returns curves. To avoid this confusion, the latter are best labelled average and marginal product curves.
- Confusing profit maximisation and revenue maximisation.
- Failing to understand the relationship between average and marginal revenue.
- Failing to understand the MR = MC profit-maximising rule, and that it identifies a firm's equilibrium level of output in all market structures: perfect competition, monopoly and oligopoly.
- Writing long, irrelevant answers on the conditions of perfect competition or the causes of monopoly, when the question requires analysis and the application of theory rather than repetition of rote-learnt material.

# Perfect competition and monopoly

These notes, which relate to AQA specification sections 14.2 and 14.3, prepare you to answer AQA examination questions on:

- short-run and long-run equilibrium in perfect competition
- monopoly equilibrium
- causes of monopoly and sources of monopoly power

## Essential information

### The equilibrium firm

**Equilibrium** is one of the most important concepts in economics. It means a state of rest or balance, in which there is no reason for anything to change unless it is disturbed, in which case **disequilibrium** replaces equilibrium. You learnt in Module 1: Markets and Market Failure that a market is in equilibrium when planned demand = planned supply. Within the market, a firm is in equilibrium when it **fulfils its market plans**, producing and selling the level of output at which MR = MC and **profit is maximised**. If the firm produces below this level of output (in which case MR > MC), then, by stepping up output, profit increases. Conversely, if the firm produces beyond the profit-maximising level of output (in which case MR < MC), then, by cutting back output, profit increases.

### Normal and supernormal profit

Before explaining the profit-maximising or equilibrium firm in perfect competition, it is necessary first to introduce **normal profit** and **supernormal profit**. (Supernormal profit is also known as **abnormal profit** and **above-normal profit**.) Normal profit is the minimum level of profit necessary to keep existing firms in production, while being insufficient to attract new firms into the market. Because a firm must make normal profit to stay in production, **economists treat normal profit as a cost of production**, including it in a firm's average cost curve. In the long run, firms unable to make normal profit leave the market. Supernormal profit is any extra profit over and above normal profit. In the long run and in the absence of entry barriers, supernormal profit performs the important economic function of attracting new firms into the market.

### Perfect competition short-run equilibrium

Figure 8 shows the equilibrium level of output produced by a perfectly competitive firm in the short run. As we saw in the previous topic, the firm (shown in the left-hand panel of the diagram) has to accept the ruling price determined by market supply and demand (shown in the right-hand panel). We also explained that the **ruling price** is also the **average revenue (AR) curve** and the **marginal revenue (MR) curve**. Using the MR = MC condition, the firm's profit-maximising or equilibrium output occurs at $Q_1$. At this level of output, total sales revenue (quantity sold times price) is shown by the area $OP_1YQ_1$. Total cost (quantity sold times average cost) is the area $OC_1ZQ_1$.

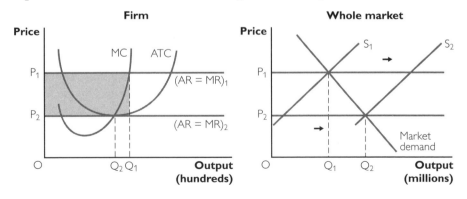

This means that supernormal profit (total revenue minus total cost) is the shaded area $C_1P_1YZ$. You should note that supernormal profit could be made at levels of output other than $Q_1$ (indeed, at all levels of output at which price is above average cost), but the profit would be less than at $Q_1$. Only by producing and selling $Q_1$ can the firm make the largest possible supernormal profit.

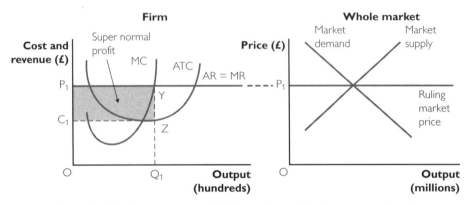

*Figure 8 The short-run equilibrium of a perfectly competitive firm*

**Perfect competition long-run equilibrium**

The short-run equilibrium shown in Figure 8 is a temporary equilibrium rather than a true equilibrium. In the short run, new firms cannot enter the market, so incumbent firms (i.e. firms already in the market) continue to make supernormal profit. However in the long run, when there are no entry barriers and firms can enter or leave the market freely, supernormal profit (shown by the shaded area in the left-hand panel of Figure 9) acts as a 'magnet', attracting new firms into the market. The entry of new firms shifts the market supply curve rightward from $S_1$ to $S_2$ in the right-hand panel of Figure 9. This causes the ruling market price to fall until it settles at $P_2$. Market and firm are now both in long-run or *true* equilibrium.

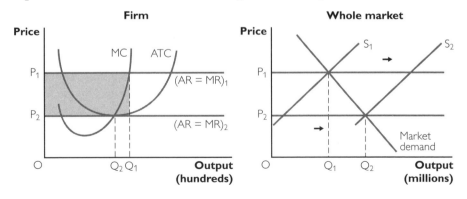

*Figure 9 How long-run equilibrium is achieved in perfect competition*

Figure 10 shows more clearly a perfectly competitive firm in long-run equilibrium. The price line just touches the lowest point of the firm's ATC curve, so no supernormal profit is made. Because surviving firms make normal profit only, the incentive for new firms to enter the market has disappeared.

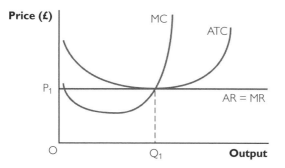

*Figure 10 A perfectly competitive firm in long-run equilibrium*

## Monopoly equilibrium

Just like a perfectly competitive firm, a monopoly maximises profit by producing the level of output at which MR = MC. In Figure 11, point A locates the profit-maximising level of output ($Q_1$), but the price charged by the monopoly is located at point D on the demand curve (and AR curve), immediately above point A. Supernormal profit (or above-normal profit) is shown by the shaded area $C_1P_1DB$. Unlike perfect competition, the diagram does not distinguish between *short-run* and *long-run* equilibrium. This is because in monopoly, **entry barriers** prevent new firms joining the market, thus enabling the monopoly to make supernormal profits in the long run as well as the short run. In contrast to perfect competition, where supernormal profits are temporary, a monopoly makes supernormal profit as long as entry barriers protect it. Indeed in monopoly, supernormal profit is often called **monopoly profit**, indicating the monopolist's power to preserve profit by preventing competition.

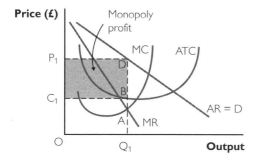

*Figure 11 Monopoly equilibrium*

## Causes of monopoly and sources of monopoly power

**Monopoly power** stems from a firm's ability to exclude rivals from the market by imposing **entry barriers**. A pure monopoly obviously possesses monopoly power, but firms in imperfectly competitive markets such as oligopolies can also exercise

monopoly power to a greater or lesser extent. Whereas perfect competition is charac-
terised by **consumer sovereignty** (the idea that the 'consumer is king', in the sense
that firms respond to the wishes of consumers exercised through their pounds spent
in the market), monopolies exercise and exploit **producer sovereignty**. Consumers
cannot go elsewhere to buy the good, and are presented with a 'take it or leave it'
choice. Enjoying producer sovereignty, a firm with monopoly power exploits
consumers by **restricting output** and **raising price** (compared to output and price in
a perfectly competitive market), by **restricting consumer choice** and by making
permanent **excess profit** (supernormal profit).

But even when a firm is a monopoly producer of a particular good or service,
monopoly power is weak if close substitutes exist, produced by other firms in other
industries. Monopoly power is greatest when the firm produces an essential good for
which there are no substitutes. Factors that give rise to monopoly power include
**advantages of geographical location**, **control over raw material supply or market
outlets, economies of scale**, the use of **advertising**, **branding** and **product differentiation** as entry barriers, and laws such as **patent legislation**, which protect innova-
tions and intellectual property from copying or 'cloning'.

### Natural monopoly
In the past, **utility industries** such as water, gas, electricity and the telephone industry
possessed great monopoly power. Because of the nature of their product, utility
industries experience a particular marketing problem. The industries produce a
service that is delivered through a distribution network or grid of pipes and cables
into millions of separate businesses and homes. Competition in the provision of
distribution grids is extremely wasteful, since it requires the duplication of fixed
capacity, therefore causing each supplier to incur unnecessarily high fixed costs. For
this reason, the utility industries were said to be **natural monopolies**: that is, industries that would be monopolies whoever owned them. Until the 1980s and 1990s,
most UK utilities such as the British Gas Corporation and BT were publicly owned
monopolies and nationalised industries. Virtually all the utilities have now been
privatised. The topic 'Industrial policy' (pp. 40–45) looks at how **regulation** and
**deregulation** are used to remove entry barriers and make the utility markets competitive and **contestable**.

## Examination questions and skills

Examination questions, usually part (a) of essay questions, are likely test the skill of
explaining and illustrating perfect competition or monopoly equilibrium. In this book,
part (a) of EQ1 should be answered by drawing and explaining a diagram to show
*either* perfect competition equilibrium or monopoly equilibrium. You do not need both.
Part (a) of EQ2 is more specific, requiring explanation of how price and output are determined in perfect competition. In contrast to part (a) of an essay question, which instructs
you to *explain*, typically part (b) asks you to *evaluate*, *assess* or *discuss*. You could
be asked to evaluate the desirable and undesirable properties of perfect competition

equilibrium and/or monopoly equilibrium. The skills needed, which relate to **efficiency concepts**, are explained in the topic 'Evaluating market structures' (pp. 34–39).

Perfect competition and monopoly do not figure explicitly in any of the data-response questions in this book, though DRQs 1 and 2 test understanding of the extent to which real-world markets (computer games and airlines) are competitive, and the methods of competition (and anti-competitive practices) used in these markets.

## Common examination errors

Commonly made mistakes on perfect competition and monopoly include the following:

- Explaining perfect competition equilibrium solely in terms of the whole market and not a firm within the market, or vice versa.
- Failing to apply correctly the MR = MC rule, particularly for monopoly equilibrium.
- Failing to distinguish between short-run and long-run equilibrium in perfect competition.
- Failing to understand normal profit and supernormal profit and to apply the concepts in analysis.
- Writing long irrelevant answers on the causes of monopoly, when the question requires explanation and analysis of monopoly equilibrium.

# Oligopoly

These notes, which relate to AQA specification section 14.3, prepare you to answer AQA examination questions on:

- the meaning of oligopoly
- competitive and collusive oligopoly
- price discrimination and other aspects of pricing in imperfect competition

## Essential information

### The meaning of oligopoly

**Oligopoly** is a **market structure** in which a few large firms dominate the market. This means there is a high degree of **market concentration**, which can be measured by a **concentration ratio**. For example, a five-firm concentration ratio of 80% means that the five largest firms produce 80% of market output.

However, oligopoly is best defined by **market conduct**, or the **behaviour of the firms within the market**, rather than by **market structure**. Oligopolists are **interdependent** rather than *independent*, in the sense that they need to take account of the likely reactions of their rivals, the other oligopolists, when making price and output decisions. Consider, for example, an oligopolist who is thinking of raising the price charged in order to increase profit. Whether the price rise succeeds in increasing profit depends upon the likely reactions of the other firms. Will rival firms follow suit and match the price rise, or will they hold their prices steady, hoping to gain sales at the expense of the firm that raised the price? Clearly, when deciding whether to raise or lower its price, an oligopolist must make assumptions about the likely response of the other firms.

Because there are a very great number of possible ways in which oligopolistic firms may react to each other's pricing and output strategies, it is impossible to construct an all-embracing oligopoly theory. The more sophisticated oligopoly models are examples of **game theory**. Each oligopolist is regarded as a player in a game, choosing a strategy to win the game by attaching statistical probabilities to various possible outcomes and to the likely retaliatory strategies adopted by its rivals. Different assumptions about the likely reaction of rivals may lead to a different pricing decision by the firm itself.

### Perfect and imperfect oligopoly

**Perfect oligopoly** exists when the oligopolists produce a uniform or homogeneous product such as petrol. By contrast, **imperfect oligopoly** occurs when the products of the oligopoly are by their nature differentiated, such as automobiles.

### Competitive and collusive oligopoly

As we have noted, in **competitive oligopoly** a firm has to take account of the reactions of its rivals when forming its market strategy, but it does so without cooperating or colluding with the other firms. **Uncertainty** is a characteristic of competitive oligopoly — a firm can never be completely certain of how rivals will react to its marketing strategy. Will they or will they not follow suit?

Uncertainty can be reduced by the rivals **cooperating** or **colluding** to fix prices or output, or even by allocating customers to particular members of the oligopoly. For example, by forming a **cartel agreement** or **price ring**, oligopolists can achieve a better outcome for them all, in terms of **joint-profit maximisation** and an easier life, than by remaining a competitive oligopoly. However, collusion or cooperative behaviour may not be good for the consumer, resulting in the **disadvantages of monopoly**, **such as high prices and restriction of choice**, without any of the **benefits, such as economies of scale**. For this reason, collusive oligopolistic arrangements such as cartel agreements are normally illegal, regarded by governments as against the public interest. In any case, it is seldom possible to eliminate uncertainty completely. Members of a cartel may cheat or renege on an agreement, secretly selling extra output at a price that undercuts the cartel's agreed price.

### The kinked demand curve theory of competitive oligopoly

The **kinked demand curve** theory, which is illustrated in Figure 12, can be used to explain a number of features of competitive oligopoly, such as interdependence, uncertainty and a preference for avoiding price wars. The theory was originally developed to explain price rigidity and the absence of price wars in oligopolistic markets. Suppose an oligopolist sells output $Q_1$ at price $P_1$ as shown in the left-hand panel of Figure 12. Because oligopolists lack accurate information about the demand and revenue curves they face, particularly at outputs other than those they are currently producing, each firm has to guess what will happen to demand if it changes its price.

The demand curve DD in Figure 12 represents an oligopolist's estimate of how demand will change with respect to either a price rise or a price fall. DD has been drawn on the assumption that the firm expects demand for its product to be relatively elastic in response to a price rise because rivals are expected to react by keeping their prices stable in the hope of gaining profits and market share. But because the oligopolist expects rivals to react to a price cut by decreasing their prices by the same amount, demand is expected to be less elastic in response to a price reduction, since few, if any, customers will be lured away from rival firms.

The oligopolist therefore **expects rival firms to react asymmetrically** when price is raised compared to when price is lowered. The oligopolist's initial price and output, $P_1$ and $Q_1$, locate the junction of two demand curves of different elasticity, each reflecting a different assumption about how rivals are expected to react to a change in price. The oligopolist expects profit to be lost whether price is raised or cut. On these assumptions, the best policy is to leave price unchanged!

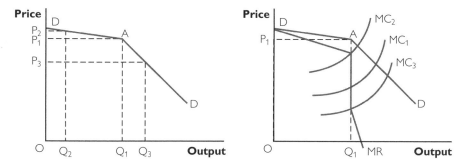

*Figure 12 The kinked demand curve theory*

The right-hand panel of Figure 12 illustrates a way in which the kinked demand curve theory can be developed further. As in all market structures, the demand curve facing an oligopolist is also its average revenue (AR) curve. But as we saw for monopoly in the topic 'Perfect competition and monopoly' (pp. 25–29), when AR falls, marginal revenue (MR) is below AR. You should note that the MR curve in Figure 12 has three sections. The uppermost section relates to the more elastic section of the AR curve to the left of the 'kink' at point A, while the lowermost section relates to the less elastic section of the AR curve below and to the right of the 'kink'. The mid-section of the MR curve is the vertical line joining the upper and lower sections of the MR curve below point A at the output level $Q_1$. Suppose the MC curve is initially $MC_1$. You should note that MR = MC at output $Q_1$, and that $P_1$ is the profit-maximising price. But you should also note that if the MC curve rises or falls between $MC_2$ and $MC_3$, the profit-maximising output and price continue to be $Q_1$ and $P_1$ respectively. The oligopolist's selling price remains stable despite quite significant changes in costs of production.

### Weaknesses of the kinked demand curve theory

Although at first sight attractive as an explanation of price stability in conditions of oligopoly, the kinked demand theory has two significant weaknesses. First, it is an incomplete theory, since it does not explain how and why a firm chooses to be at point A in the first place. Second, evidence provided by the pricing decisions of real-world firms gives little support to the theory. Rival firms seldom respond to price changes in the manner assumed in the kinked demand curve theory, and it is also reasonable to expect that an oligopolist would test the market: that is, raise or lower the selling price to see if rivals react in the manner expected. If the rivals did not, then the oligopolist would surely revise its estimate of demand for its product. Evidence conclusively shows that oligopoly prices tend to be stable or sticky when demand conditions change in a predictable or cyclical way, and that oligopolists usually raise or lower prices quickly and by significant amounts, both when production costs change substantially and when unexpected shifts in demand occur.

### Non-price competition

The kinked demand curve theory suggests that oligopolists are reluctant to use **price competition** to gain sales and market share, although there is plenty of evidence that oligopolists do on occasion engage in **price wars**, even though, according to the kinked demand theory, such wars are self-defeating. Nevertheless, oligopolists also engage in many forms of **non-price competition**, such as **marketing competition** (for example, obtaining exclusive outlets such as tied public houses and petrol stations through which breweries and oil companies can sell their products), the use of **persuasive advertising**, **product differentiation, brand imaging** and **packaging**, and **quality competition**, including the **provision of after-sales service**.

### Price discrimination

Oligopolists (and monopolists) sometimes use **price discrimination** to increase their profits. Price discrimination occurs when firms charge different prices to different customers based on differences in the customers' ability and willingness to pay. Those customers who are prepared to pay more are charged a higher price than those who are only willing to pay a lower price. It is important to understand that discriminatory prices are for the most part based on differences in demand conditions rather than on differences in costs of production. You should refer to the answer to part (c) of DRQ1 in the Questions and Answers section of this guide for further explanation of price discrimination.

### Other aspects of pricing in imperfect competition

Imperfectly competitive firms (and also monopolies) set prices in several different ways.

- **Cost-plus pricing**, also known as **mark-up pricing** and **full-cost pricing**, is a commonly used pricing rule. Cost-plus pricing means that a firm sets its selling price by adding a standard percentage profit margin to average or unit costs.
- **Price leadership** is also common in oligopoly, perhaps because overt collusive agreements to fix the market price, such as cartel agreements, are usually illegal. Price leadership occurs when one firm becomes the market leader and other firms in the industry follow its pricing example.
- **Limit pricing** and **predatory pricing** are two forms of pricing undertaken by dominant firms in markets where 'natural' entry barriers are low or non-existent. In the case of **limit pricing**, a dominant firm realises that if it sets the **short-run profit-maximising price**, the entry of new firms will quickly erode its supernormal profit. To prevent this happening, the dominant firm sets a deliberately low price (the limit price) to deter entry by new firms. The firm sacrifices short-term profits that a higher price would yield in order to **maximise long-run profits**, achieved through preventing or limiting the entry of new firms. Limit pricing, which is legal, is related to the **theory of contestable markets** (see the topic 'Industrial policy', pp. 40–45). In contrast to limit pricing, which deters market entry, successful **predatory pricing** removes recent entrants to the market. Predatory pricing occurs when an incumbent firm deliberately **sets prices below cost** to force new market entrants out of business. Once the new entrants have left the market and its dominance has been restored, the firm will restore prices to their previous profit-maximising level. Predatory pricing is an **anti-competitive trading restrictive practice** (see 'Industrial policy', pp. 40–45), and is therefore illegal.

## Examination questions and skills

Virtually every real-world market is imperfectly competitive, so it is easy for chief examiners to find source material on oligopoly that is suitable for a data-response question. The compulsory DRQ in the Unit 5 examination has often been set on an imperfectly competitive market. (By contrast, perfect competition and monopoly are more likely to be tested by essay questions because it is less easy to find suitable real-world data on these market structures.) DRQs 1 and 2 in this book, which are respectively on the computer games and airline markets, test knowledge and understanding of oligopoly.

The kinked demand curve theory is unlikely to figure explicitly in a question. Questions will, however, be set on the behaviour of oligopolistic firms. If properly used and applied, the kinked demand curve theory can be used to explain and analyse many aspects of competitive oligopoly: for example, how firms are affected by interdependence and uncertainty, and why oligopolists may prefer non-price competition to price competition. Part (b) of DRQ1 requires explanation of limit pricing and predatory pricing, while to answer part (c), you must analyse price discrimination. Part (c) of DRQ2 asks for analysis of how large airlines may compete against new entrant budget carriers such as easyJet.

## Common examination errors

Commonly made mistakes on perfect competition and monopoly include the following:
- Imprecise descriptions of market structure and concentration.
- Defining oligopoly solely in terms of market structure rather than the firms' inter-dependence.
- Failing to understand why oligopolists may wish to collude.
- Inaccurately drawn diagrams and inaccurate written explanation of the kinked demand curve theory.
- Failing to understand the theory of price discrimination.
- Writing 'all the candidate knows' about the kinked demand curve theory, when the question requires selective application of theory to the issue posed by the question.

# Evaluating market structures

These notes, which relate to AQA specification sections 14.2 and 14.3, prepare you to answer AQA examination questions on applying:
- efficiency concepts to evaluate market structures
- welfare concepts to evaluate market structures

## Essential information

### The meaning of economic efficiency

Any economic decision or course of action (by an individual, a firm or the government) is **efficient** if it achieves the economic agent's desired objective at minimum cost to the agent, and with minimum undesired side-effects or distortion. More specifically, how well or badly a market performs depends in part on its **efficiency**. A number of different efficiency concepts are used to evaluate market performance. Those in the Module 5 specification are **productive efficiency, allocative efficiency, static efficiency** and **dynamic efficiency**. Although not in the specification (and therefore not figuring explicitly in Unit 5 examination questions), two other efficiency concepts will be considered: **technical efficiency** and **X-efficiency**.

### Technical efficiency

A production process is **technically efficient** if it *maximises* the output of a good produced from given or available inputs. Alternatively, it can be said that for a particular level of output, a production process is technically efficient if it *minimises* the inputs of capital and labour required to produce that level of output.

### Productive efficiency

Whereas technical efficiency is defined in terms of the relationship in production between inputs and outputs, **productive efficiency** (or **cost efficiency**) is usually measured in terms of money costs of production. Productive efficiency requires that output is produced at the lowest possible average cost. In the *short run*, the productively efficient level of output occurs at the lowest point on the firm's short-run ATC curve. For the firm shown in Figure 13, the productively efficient level of output is $Q_1$, where average costs are minimised at $C_1$.

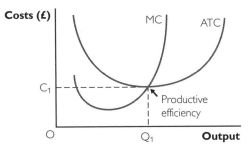

**Figure 13 Productive efficiency**

But in the *long run*, the most productively efficient of *all* the firm's possible levels of output is produced at the lowest point on the firm's long-run average cost (LRATC) curve, at the **scale** or size of firm that minimises unit costs. **Remember also that the economy as a whole is productively efficient — and also technically efficient — when it is producing on its production possibility frontier.**

## X-efficiency

X-inefficiency occurs whenever, for any particular scale of fixed capacity and level of production, the firm incurs **unnecessary production costs**: that is, it could in principle reduce costs. There are two causes of X-inefficiency: combining factors of production in a technically inefficient way to produce a particular level of output (for example, 'over-manning' and continuously idle machinery); and paying workers or managers unnecessarily high wages or salaries, or buying raw materials or capital at unnecessarily high prices. A firm is producing **X-efficiently** when, given its size or available capacity, it eliminates all unnecessary costs of production. The firm shown in Figure 14 is X-inefficient if it produces output $Q_1$ at an average cost of $C_2$ (that is, the firm is producing above its average cost curve at point X). By contrast, if the firm produces on its average cost curve (at $C_1$), it is X-efficient. All points on the ATC curve are X-efficient.

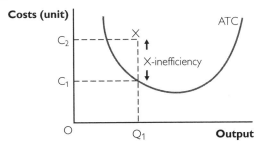

**Figure 14 X-efficiency and X-inefficiency**

### Allocative efficiency

Allocative efficiency relates to how the goods produced from the economy's scarce resources are used: that is, how they are allocated between final uses. As a generalisation, allocative efficiency occurs when the best combination of goods is produced. An economy is said to be allocatively efficient when it is impossible to allocate final goods so as to make one person better off without at the same time making another person worse off. A necessary condition for a market economy to be allocatively efficient is that the prices of all goods must equal their marginal costs of production: $P = MC$ throughout the economy. A particular market is allocatively efficient if, in that market, $P = MC$. Strictly, however, prices must also equal relevant marginal costs in all other markets in the economy.

### Static efficiency

All the efficiency types considered so far are forms of **static efficiency**. Static efficiency side-steps the fact that the economy is constantly changing, with new technologies, methods of production and final goods being developed and economic growth taking place.

### Dynamic efficiency

By contrast with static efficiency, **dynamic efficiency** results from **improvements in technical and productive efficiency that occur over time**. A dynamically efficient economy is proficient at improving methods of producing existing products, and also at developing and marketing completely new products. In both cases, **invention**, **innovation** and **research and development (R & D)** can lead to significant improvements in dynamic efficiency.

### Evaluating perfect competition and monopoly in terms of economic efficiency

The left-hand and right-hand panels of Figure 15 respectively show a perfectly competitive firm and a monopoly in equilibrium — assuming that firms in both markets have similar ATC curves. This means there are **no economies of scale**. The diagram shows that the perfectly competitive firm is productively efficient (producing where ATC are lowest), but that monopoly is productively inefficient (producing above minimum ATC). Likewise, the perfectly competitive firm is allocatively efficient (as $P = MC$), whereas the monopoly charges a higher price and produces at a lower output than is allocatively efficient ($P > MC$).

In long-run equilibrium, a perfectly competitive firm must also be X-efficient. The reason is simple. If the firm is X-inefficient, incurring unnecessary costs, the firm could not make normal profits in the long run. To survive or make normal profits, the firm must take action to eliminate 'organisational slack' or X-inefficiency. Because of the absence of competitive pressures, which in perfect competition serve to eliminate supernormal profit, monopoly may also be X-inefficient. A monopoly can often survive, happily incurring unnecessary production costs and making 'satisfactory' rather than 'maximum' profits, because the absence or weakness of competitive forces means that there is no mechanism in monopoly to eliminate X-inefficiency.

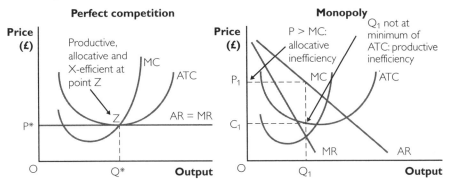

*Figure 15 Evaluating perfect competition and monopoly in terms of economic efficiency*

However, **the conclusion that perfect competition is productively more efficient than monopoly depends on an assumption that there are no economies of scale**. When substantial economies of scale are possible in an industry, monopoly may be productively more efficient than competition. Figure 16 illustrates a **natural monopoly** where, because of limited market size, there is no room in the market for more than one firm benefiting from full economies of scale. Producing on the short-run average cost curve $SRATC_N$, the monopoly may be producing above the lowest point on this particular cost curve, hence exhibiting a degree of productive inefficiency. However, *all* points on $SRATC_N$ incur lower unit costs — and are productively *more* efficient — than any point on $SRATC_1$, which is the relevant cost curve for each firm if the monopoly is broken into a number of smaller competitive enterprises.

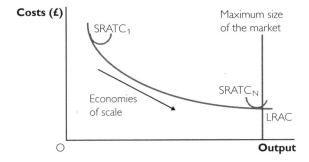

*Figure 16 The justification of monopoly when economies of scale are possible*

Under certain circumstances, monopolies may also be more **dynamically efficient** than a perfectly competitive firm. Because it is protected by entry barriers, a monopoly earns monopoly profit without facing the threat that the profit will be whittled away as new firms enter the market. This allows an innovating monopoly to enjoy the fruits of successful R & D and product development in the form of monopoly profit. In perfect competition, by contrast, there is little or no incentive to innovate because other firms can 'free ride' and gain costless access to the results of any successful research. This argument is used to justify **patent legislation**, which grants a firm the right to exploit the monopoly position created by innovation for a number of years before the patent expires.

However, there is a counter-argument that monopoly reduces rather than promotes innovation and dynamic efficiency. As noted earlier, protected from competitive pressures, a monopoly may **profit satisfice** rather than *profit maximise*, content with satisfactory profits and an easy life.

### Evaluating perfect competition and monopoly in terms of economic welfare

To explain how market structures affect **economic welfare**, we must first introduce the concepts of consumer surplus and producer surplus as measures of welfare. **Consumer surplus** and **producer surplus** are illustrated in Figure 17.

Consumer surplus is the difference between the *maximum* price a consumer is prepared to pay and the *actual price he or she need pay*. In a competitive market such as the left-hand side of Figure 17, the total consumer surplus enjoyed by all the consumers in the market is measured by the triangular area $P_1EA$. Consumer welfare increases whenever consumer surplus increases: for example, when market prices fall. Conversely, however, higher prices reduce consumer surplus and welfare.

Producer surplus, which is a measure of producers' welfare, is the difference between the *minimum price* a firm is prepared to charge for a good and the *actual price charged*. In the left-hand side of Figure 17, the producer surplus enjoyed by all the firms in the market is measured by the triangular area $FP_1A$.

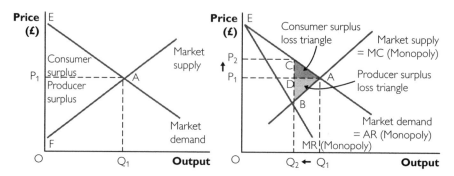

*Figure 17 Market structure and economic welfare*

The right-hand side of Figure 17 illustrates what happens to economic welfare when monopoly replaces perfect competition (assuming there are no economies of scale). Market equilibrium in perfect competition is determined at point A: output is $Q_1$ and price is $P_1$. However, monopoly equilibrium is determined at point B, where MR = MC. (Note that the marginal cost curve in monopoly is the same curve as market supply in perfect competition.) The diagram illustrates the standard case against monopoly, namely that compared to perfect competition, monopoly restricts output (to $Q_2$) and raises price (to $P_2$). But we can take the analysis one stage further and investigate how consumer surplus and producer surplus (and hence economic welfare) are affected. Raising the price from $P_1$ to $P_2$ transfers consumer surplus equal to the rectangular area $P_1 P_2 CD$ to the monopoly. This means that producer surplus (in the form of monopoly profit) increases at the expense of consumer surplus. Over and above this transfer, however, there is a **net loss of economic welfare** caused by the fact that the amount bought and sold falls to $Q_2$. The welfare loss is shown by the two shaded triangular areas taken together, which respectively depict the loss of consumer surplus and the loss of producer surplus.

## Examination questions and skills

Part (a) of EQ3 tests knowledge and understanding of the different types of economic efficiency explained in this topic, in the context of monopoly. Efficiency concepts are also relevant for explaining and analysing the issues posed by parts (b) of EQ1 and EQ2. Takeovers and mergers (the subject of part (b) of EQ1) may lead to monopoly and to the various inefficiencies and efficiencies associated with monopoly. A good answer to part (b) of EQ2 might argue that, although perfect competition is an abstract and unrealistic market structure, it provides a benchmark or yardstick for evaluating productive and allocative inefficiency (and welfare losses and gains) in real-world imperfectly competitive markets.

This topic has explained economic efficiency and economic welfare in the context of the two extreme market structures of perfect competition and monopoly. You might also be required to use the concepts to explain, analyse and evaluate firms' behaviour and performance in imperfectly competitive markets lying between these two extremes. For example, welfare loss (and transfer of consumer surplus) is relevant to part (c) of DRQ1, in the context of possible price discrimination undertaken by oligopolistic firms in the computer games industry.

## Common examination errors

Commonly made mistakes on evaluating market structures include the following:
- Confusing the different types of economic efficiency.
- Failing to understand allocative efficiency.
- Confusing efficiency with equity.
- Inability to apply efficiency concepts to analyse the properties of perfect competition equilibrium and monopoly equilibrium.
- Wrongly arguing that perfect competition is efficient and monopoly is inefficient because entrepreneurs in perfectly competitive markets take account of the public interest and do not pursue their private self-interests.
- Failing to appreciate the economies of scale and dynamic efficiency justifications of monopoly.
- Failing to understand and apply the concepts of economic welfare, consumer surplus and producer surplus.

# Industrial policy

These notes, which relate to AQA specification section 14.5, prepare you to answer AQA examination questions on:

- competition policy
- public ownership and privatisation
- regulation and deregulation of markets

## Essential information

### Industrial policy and competition policy

**Industrial policy** is part of the government's **microeconomic policy**, which aims to improve the economic performance of individual economic agents, firms and industries on the supply side of the economy. Industrial policy therefore provides examples of **supply-side economic policies**.

Since its beginnings in 1948, **competition policy** has been an important part of UK industrial policy. Competition policy is the part of industrial policy that covers **monopolies**, **mergers** and **restrictive trading practices**.

### Monopoly policy

UK policy identifies two types of monopoly known as scale monopoly and complex monopoly. **Scale monopoly** occurs when one firm has at least 25% of the market, whereas a **complex monopoly** exists when a number of firms together have a 25% share and conduct their affairs so as to restrict competition.

By comparison to perfect competition, **monopoly may reduce output and raise prices**, thus **promoting productive and allocative inefficiency**. Monopolies may also **exploit their producer sovereignty** by manipulating consumer wants and restricting choice, and by **price discriminating** between different groups of customers. However, the key argument against monopoly — that dominant firms use market power to restrict output and raise prices — depends crucially upon the assumption that firms of different size all have similar cost curves. In industries where **economies of large-scale production** are possible, this is not the case. The existence of economies of scale means that large firms can benefit from lower costs and achieve a more productively efficient outcome than smaller firms, and monopolies may also be more **dynamically efficient**.

In the past, **utility industries** such as gas, water and electricity supply, sewage disposal, telecommunications and postal services were regarded as **natural monopolies**. The key question was: should natural monopolies be organised as **nationalised industries**, or should they be left in private hands, but subject to strong and effective public **regulation**?

UK competition policy has generally recognised that monopoly can be good or bad depending upon circumstances. It has adopted the pragmatic view that each case of monopoly must be judged on its merits. If the likely costs resulting from the reduction of competition exceed the benefits, monopoly should be prevented. But if the likely benefits exceed the costs, monopoly should be permitted, provided the monopoly does not abuse its position and exploit the consuming public.

UK monopoly policy is implemented by the **Office of Fair Trading (OFT)** and the **Competition Commission**, which are responsible to a government ministry, the **Department of Trade and Industry (DTI)**. The OFT uses **market structure, conduct** and **performance indicators** to scan or screen the UK economy on a systematic basis for evidence of monopoly abuse. **Concentration ratios** provide evidence of monopolistic market structures, while market conduct indicators, such as consumer and trade complaints and evidence of **price discrimination**, **price leadership** and **merger activity**, allow the OFT to monitor anti-competitive business behaviour. The performance indicators used to measure business efficiency include price movements and changes in profit margins.

When the OFT discovers evidence of statutory monopoly which it believes is likely to be against the public interest, it refers the firms involved to the Competition Commission for further investigation. The Competition Commission interprets the public interest largely in terms of the effect upon competitiveness of the trading practices it is asked to investigate. Following an investigation, the Competition Commission reports its findings to the DTI, which may then: implement some or all of the recommendations; shelve the report and do nothing; or take action completely contrary to the commission's advice!

In fact, the government has quite wide powers to take action on receipt of the Competition Commission's recommendations. In extreme cases, the DTI can issue an order requiring firms to split up or sell off assets. In practice, however, these order-making powers are seldom used.

Although a **cost–benefit** approach which involves **taking each case on its merits** is central to UK monopoly policy, there are a number of other possible approaches to the problems posed by monopoly. These include the following:
- **The compulsory breaking up of all monopolies**. Some economists believe that only when the economy resembles perfect competition will the advantages of a free-market economy, namely economic efficiency and consumer sovereignty, be achieved. Monopoly must be regarded as bad and can never be justified. This approach suggests the adoption of an automatic policy rule to break up existing monopolies.
- **Price controls**. These are used in the form of the **RPI–X price cap** imposed on privatised utility companies such as BT.
- **Taxing monopoly profits** to encourage monopolies to reduce prices and profits.
- **Public ownership**. Labour governments have sometimes regarded the problem of monopoly as resulting from private ownership and the pursuit of private profit. They nationalised monopolies in the belief that state-owned monopolies act in the public interest.

- **Privatisation**. In contrast to the socialist view that the problem of monopoly stems in large part from private ownership and the profit motive, free-market economists believe that state ownership produces abuses, such as a feather-bedded workforce protected from any form of market discipline. They argue that privatisation improves efficiency and commercial performance because it exposes firms to the threat of takeover and market discipline.
- **Removing barriers to entry**. Privatisation alone cannot end monopoly abuse, since it merely changes the nature of the problem back to private monopoly and the commercial exploitation of a monopoly position. Entry barriers must also be removed to make the market contestable.

A market is **contestable** if the **potential** exists for firms to enter and leave the market without incurring entry or exit costs. In particular, there must be no or few **sunk costs**. Sunk costs are costs incurred when a firm enters a market, which it cannot recover if it decides to leave. Huge sums spent on advertising and promotion, which are irrecoverable if the firm fails to penetrate the market and decides to cut its losses and leave, are a sunk cost. A complete absence of sunk costs and entry barriers means that a market is **perfectly contestable**. Such markets may attract **hit and run entrants**: that is, new firms that enter the market, make a quick profit and then leave.

Modern monopoly policy centres on making markets contestable by removing entry and exit barriers and trying to reduce sunk costs. Actual contestability is not required, only **potential contestability**. A dominant firm may survive in a contestable market by setting **limit prices** (see p. 33).

The theory of contestable markets suggests that monopoly should be defined, not by the number of firms in the market or by concentration ratios, but rather by the potential ease or difficulty with which new firms may enter the market. Monopoly is not regarded as a problem, even if there is only one established firm in the market, providing that an absence of barriers to entry and exit creates the *potential* for new firms to enter and contest the market. This is sufficient, according to the contestable market theory, to ensure efficient and non-exploitative behaviour by existing firms within the market. Government intervention should be restricted to discovering which industries and markets are potentially contestable, and then using **regulatory** and **deregulatory policies** to develop conditions, through the removal of barriers to entry and exit, to ensure that contestability is possible.

## Merger policy

**Merger policy** is concerned with takeovers and acquisitions that might create a monopoly situation. As with the part of competition policy that deals with already established monopolies and concentrated markets, UK merger policy reflects the influence of the **theory of contestable markets**. Currently a merger is only usually referred for investigation by the Competition Commission if the OFT believes the merger might have significant anti-competitive effects. Lateral or diversifying mergers or takeovers are not usually investigated, nor are takeovers by overseas-based multinational companies.

Critics believe that UK merger policy is much too weak and ineffective. However, the ability of a UK government to toughen its merger policy is limited by the fact that many mergers involving UK companies fall under the remit of European Union competition policy. Under the EU principle of **subsidiarity**, which delegates policy as much as possible to national governments, UK national policy deals with smaller mergers, but the European Commission adjudicates on larger mergers with an EU dimension.

### Policy towards restrictive trading practices

**Restrictive trading practices** undertaken by firms in imperfectly competitive markets divide into those undertaken independently by a single firm, and collective restrictive practices that involve an agreement or collusion between two or more firms. The former include **refusal to supply** and **full-line forcing**, whereby a supplier forces a distributor that wishes to sell one of the supplier's products to stock the full range of its products. Such practices are often considered as evidence of anti-competitive market conduct or behaviour when the OFT decides on monopoly references. By contrast, **collective restrictive agreements and practices**, such as **cartel agreements** (price rings), when discovered, are referred by the OFT to a court of law, the **Restrictive Practice Court (RPC)**. The RPC has the full power and independence of a high court. Firms found guilty of illegal collusion are fined, though not as heavily as when they fall foul of EU cartel policy. Many economists believe that UK policy towards anti-competitive restrictive trading practices should be made much tougher.

Not all collective agreements and acts of collusion between firms are anti-competitive and against the public interest. **Collective training schemes** for workers and **jointly undertaken research and development (R & D)** respectively lead to better **human and non-human capital**, thereby contributing to **improvements in dynamic efficiency.**

### Public ownership and privatisation

In the past, industries have been **nationalised** (taken into public ownership) to deal with the problem of natural monopoly and to give the government control of the key industries (or commanding heights of the economy), deemed vital for the planning of the economy. The 1950s to the 1970s were the decades of the **mixed economy**, when the major political parties agreed that a mix of public and private enterprise worked and was right for the UK. But this consensus broke down around 1980, and since then successive UK governments have followed a policy of **economic liberalisation**, two of whose elements are **privatisation** and **deregulation**.

**Privatisation** involves the transfer of ownership, usually by sale, of industries and other assets from the **public sector** to the **private sector**. Free-market economists believe that by exposing firms and industries to the discipline of the market (the capital market as well as the market in which the privatised firm sells its output), privatisation improves efficiency and economic performance. Free-marketers also argue that, by extending share ownership to individuals and employees, privatisation promotes **popular capitalism** and an **enterprise culture**. Privatisation also raises revenue for the government, which reduces, at least in the short run, the government's need to borrow.

Deregulation is the opposite of regulation. **Regulation** restricts economic agents' freedom of action in the marketplace. By removing previously imposed rules and constraints, **deregulation** increases people's freedom to pursue their self-interest. Free-market economists argue that many regulations are unnecessary, creating bureaucracy and 'red tape', which raise business costs and render firms uncompetitive. Regulation can also be an **entry barrier**, protecting the monopoly power of firms already in the market. Finally, regulation can lead to a process known as **regulatory capture**. Regulatory capture allegedly occurs when a regulator (for example, an agency regulating a privatised utility industry) 'goes native' and acts in the interest of the powerful firms that it is supposed to constrain, rather than in the interest of the consumers that it is meant to protect. Nevertheless, many regulations — for example, health and safety regulations — are undoubtedly necessary. Great harm would occur if *all* regulations and protective laws were abolished or repealed.

Other policies of economic liberalisation used in conjunction with privatisation and deregulation include contractualisation, competitive tendering, the private finance initiative and marketisation. **Contractualisation**, which is closely related to privatisation, occurs when public sector organisations such as NHS hospitals contract out the provision of services such as catering to private sector firms. The taxpayer may still pick up the bill, but private sector firms provide the service. **Competitive tendering** goes one stage further. Private sector firms tender (that is, compete) for public sector business and contracts are awarded to the firms that appear to offer best value for money. Under the **private finance initiative (PFI)**, part of the cost of major public sector investment projects is financed by the private sector, thereby saving taxpayers' money (at least in the short term). **Marketisation** (or **commercialisation**) switches the provision of goods or services from the **non-market sector** (financed by taxation) to the **market sector** (financed by sales revenue). Do not confuse *marketisation* with *privatisation* (which switches provision from the public sector to the private sector).

## Examination questions and skills

Part (b) of EQ3 centres on the theory of contestable markets in the context of monopoly. This topic has concentrated on explaining the rationale and strategy of UK competition policy, though reference has also been made to EU competition policy implemented by the EU competition commissioner. Candidates taking the Unit 4 case study paper (the alternative to Unit 4 coursework assessment) need to be familiar with the relationship between UK national competition policy and European Union competition policy. EU competition policy may provide the topic for a future case study question in the Unit 4 examination.

## Common examination errors

Commonly made mistakes on industrial policy include the following:
- Confusing scale monopoly (25% of the market) with pure monopoly (100% of the market).

- Writing a historical account of UK competition policy rather than analysing and evaluating the effectiveness of current policy.
- Failing to appreciate the cost–benefit approach of UK monopoly policy.
- Lack of awareness of alternative approaches to the problems posed by monopolies and market concentration.
- Confusing policy towards established monopoly with policy towards mergers that might create a new monopoly.
- Writing a historical account of UK privatisation rather than analysing and evaluating the advantages and disadvantages of privatisation and/or the track record of a privatised industry.
- Confusing privatisation with related policies such as marketisation and de-regulation.

# Market failure and government failure

These notes, which relate to AQA specification section 14.5, prepare you to answer AQA examination questions on:
- market failure
- cost–benefit analysis
- government failure

## Essential information

### AS and A2 specification coverage of market failure and government failure
**Market failure** and **government failure** feature in both the AS Module 1 and the A2 Module 5 specifications. These notes only cover the extra knowledge and understanding required by the Module 5 specification. They do not repeat the basic knowledge that the Unit 1: Markets and Market Failure examination assesses. You should refer to *Student Unit Guide 1*, pp. 33–42, to refresh your basic knowledge of the following market failures: **public goods**, **externalities**, **merit goods** and **demerit goods**; and for an introduction to government failure.

### The meaning of market failure
Market failure occurs whenever the market mechanism or price mechanism performs unsatisfactorily. Sometimes markets perform **inequitably**: for example, when unregulated market forces produce extreme inequalities in the distributions of income and wealth, which most people would deem **unfair** or **unjust**. The other market failures you are expected to know result from the market mechanism performing **inefficiently**.

### Monopoly and market failure
**Monopoly** and **imperfectly competitive** markets such as **oligopoly** provide examples of market failure resulting from markets performing inefficiently. The *wrong* quantity

is produced in monopoly, being sold at the *wrong* price. Compared to perfect competition (assuming no economies of scale), too little is produced which is sold at too high a price, and the market outcome is both **allocatively and productively inefficient**.

### Public goods

You learnt when studying markets and market failure at AS that **public goods** provide examples of market failure resulting from **missing markets**. The missing market results from the **non-excludability** property of a **pure public good**. It is impossible to provide pure public goods to customers who are prepared to pay, while excluding the benefits from those who are not prepared to pay. Withdrawing the benefits from one means withdrawing them from all. Each individual faces the temptation to consume without paying, or to **free ride**. If sufficient potential customers choose to free ride, the public good cannot be provided at a profit through the market. The market fails completely.

Most public goods such as roads are **non-pure public goods** rather than pure public goods, because it is possible to exclude free-riders. Roads can be converted into private goods, provided for profit through the market, by constructing toll gates, or by introducing a scheme of electronic road pricing. But even though non-pure public goods can be provided through the market, the second property of a public good, **non-rivalry**, creates a strong case for **free non-market provision**, usually by the state, with the goods being paid for collectively out of general taxation. Non-rivalry (or **non-diminishability** and **non-exhaustibility**) means that whenever an extra person consumes a public good, the benefits available to other people are not reduced. As a result, the **marginal cost of providing the good to an extra user is zero**. As **allocative efficiency** requires that $P = MC$, the allocatively efficient level of consumption of a public good occurs when $P = 0$. But market provision requires $P > 0$ to create a market-based incentive, namely profit, for entrepreneurs to provide the good. If $P > 0$, the price charged must also be greater than marginal cost ($P > MC$), which is allocatively inefficient, resulting in too low a level of consumption. Thus, even when public goods can be provided by the market, there is a case for free provision to ensure the allocatively efficient level of consumption.

### Externalities

An **externality** or **spin-off effect** is a special type of public good (or public bad) which is dumped by those who produce it on **third parties** (people who receive or consume it, whether or not they choose to). Whenever externalities result from market activity, **divergences between private and social cost and benefit** occur, which in turn cause market failure. Economists usually assume that, in a market situation, an economic agent considers only its private costs and benefits, ignoring any external costs and benefits imposed on others. **Households and firms seek to maximise their private self-interest**, and not the wider **social interest** of the whole community. When externalities are generated, costs or benefits are inevitably imposed on others, so **private benefit maximisation no longer coincides with social benefit maximisation**.

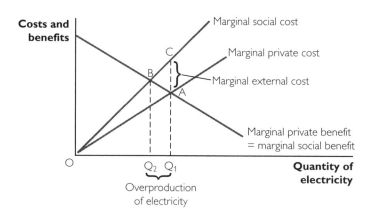

**Figure 18 Negative externalities as a cause of market failure**

Such a divergence between private and social cost and benefit is illustrated in Figure 18, which shows what happens when a power station generates **negative production externalities**, such as acid rain pollution. Assuming there are no positive externalities, the **marginal private benefit (MPB)** accruing to the power station from the production of electricity and the **marginal social benefit (MSB)** received by the whole community are the same. But because a negative externality (pollution) is discharged in the course of production, the **marginal social cost (MSC)** of production exceeds the **marginal private cost (MPC)** incurred by the power station. **Marginal external cost (MEC)** is the difference between MSC and MPC. At each level of output:

$$MSC = MPC + MEC$$

Left to itself, the power station chooses to produce and sell $Q_1$ electricity, maximising private benefit at the output determined at point A, where MPB = MPC. But the socially optimal level of output $Q_2$ is lower, being determined at point B, where MSB = MSC.

Consider also a situation in which power stations charge a price for electricity equal to the marginal *private* cost of production (P = MPC). At first sight this might appear to be allocatively efficient. But *true* allocative efficiency occurs when price equals the marginal *social* cost of production (P = MSC). P = MPC is allocatively efficient only in the absence of externalities. If negative externalities such as pollution are discharged in the course of production, setting price equal to marginal *private* cost brings about an outcome in which P < MSC. The market produces too much electricity and too much pollution. Part of the *true* cost of producing electricity, the cost of pollution, is dumped in the atmosphere and evaded by the power station. Electricity ends up being too cheap, resulting in over-consumption and over-production. The market produces the wrong or allocatively inefficient quantity of electricity.

Figure 19 extends the analysis to cover the situation in which a firm (such as a commercial forestry company) generates only **positive production externalities**. If there are no negative externalities, the MSC of tree production is the same as the MPC. But trees provide positive externalities, perhaps most significantly through water

retention and absorption of greenhouse or global-warming gases from the atmosphere. Thus the MSB for the whole community resulting from tree planting exceeds
the MPB of the commercial forestry company. At each level of output, **marginal
external benefit (MEB)** is the difference between MSB and MPB. The relationship is:

MSB = MPB + MEB

Pursuing private benefit maximisation, the commercial forestry produces at point X
in Figure 19. However the privately optimal output $Q_1$ is less than the socially optimal
output $Q_2$, located at point Y where MSB = MSC. When positive production externalities are generated, the market fails because too little of the good is produced and
consumed. Again the outcome is allocatively inefficient.

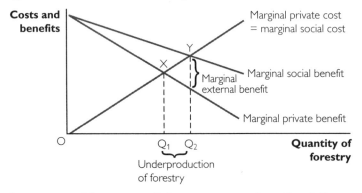

*Figure 19 Positive externalities as a cause of market failure*

When externalities are generated, **public policy** can try to ensure the correct level of
production and consumption of the good, namely the level at which MSB = MSC. This
can be done either by **quantity control** (or **regulation**), or by **taxation** and **subsidy**,
or by combining both methods. Quantity controls or regulations can influence directly
the quantity of an externality that a firm or household must generate. By contrast,
taxes and subsidies affect the information conveyed by prices (the **signalling** function
of prices), and the **incentives** that market prices create. When a **pollution tax** is set
equal to the estimated money cost of pollution, and is raised or lowered according to
the amount of pollution emitted, polluters have an incentive to pollute less. The tax,
based on the **polluter must pay** principle, **internalises the externality**. If the tax is
set so that the price the consumer pays equals MSC, an allocatively efficient level of
production and consumption may be achieved. Likewise, a tree-planting subsidy
creates an incentive to grow more trees and to produce more external benefits.

Another way of dealing with the problem of missing markets in externalities is to
use the law to **extend property rights**. This would give people the legal right to
breathe unpolluted air. If this right were breached, the victims could sue polluting
companies for financial compensation. Polluters might also offer people money to
sign away the right to breathe unpolluted air. Either way, the people who suffered
pollution would get financial compensation. (Now read the candidate's answer to
EQ4 in the Questions and Answers section of this guide. This explains a further

method of dealing with the problem of missing markets in externalities: creating a market in **permits to pollute**.)

## Merit goods and demerit goods

Merit goods and demerit goods provide further examples of divergence between private and social costs and benefits, and of the generation of externalities. In the case of a **merit good** such as education or health care, the social benefits of consumption to the whole community exceed the private benefits to the individual consumer. This is because positive externalities are generated, which benefit the wider community.

The tendency for merit goods to be under-consumed at market prices is illustrated in Figure 20(a). In the absence of regulation or subsidy, people choose to consume $Q_1$ of the merit good, maximising private benefit where MPB = MPC. However, because the social benefits of consumption exceed the private benefits, the socially optimal level of production and consumption of the merit good is $Q_2$, where MSB = MSC. Public policy needs to increase consumption from $Q_1$ to $Q_2$. As in the case of external benefits, which Figure 20(a) closely resembles, consumption can be encouraged by regulation or subsidy.

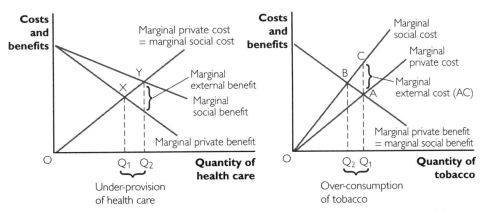

(a) How a market under–provides a merit good such as health care

(b) How a market over–provides a demerit good such as tobacco

*Figure 20 Merit and demerit goods*

As their name suggests, **demerit goods** are the opposite of merit goods. The social costs to the whole community which result from the consumption of a demerit good such as tobacco or alcohol exceed the private costs incurred by the consumer. In the same way as consumption of merit goods generates positive externalities for society as a whole, consumption of demerit goods causes negative externalities to be dumped on others. As Figure 20(b) shows, when available only at market prices, too much of a demerit good such as tobacco is consumed. The socially optimal amount of tobacco consumption is $Q_2$, located at point B where MSB = MSC. However, at market prices people choose to smoke $Q_1$ quantity of cigarettes, located at point A where MPB = MPC.

Note that the diagram indicates that *some* smoking is socially optimal. There may, of course, be more extreme situations in which the social costs resulting from the consumption of the demerit good are so severe that none should be consumed. When this is true, as may be the case for hard drugs such as heroin and cocaine, the state may discourage consumption by criminalising production or consumption, or both. But take care to avoid confusing a *demerit good* such as a narcotic drug with an economic *bad*. Remember, a bad yields only disutility or unpleasantness to the consumer, whereas a drug user certainly gains utility, at least in the short run, from his or her habit.

A tax's effectiveness in discouraging consumption of a demerit good depends both on the size of the tax and on the price elasticity of demand for the good. Because of their addictive nature, demand for demerit goods is often inelastic. This limits the tax's effectiveness in discouraging consumption.

### Cost–benefit analysis

**Cost–benefit analysis (CBA)** is a technique for evaluating *all* the costs and benefits of any economic action or decision: that is, the *social* costs and benefits to the whole community and not just the *private* costs and benefits accruing to the economic agent undertaking the action. In the past, CBA has most often been used by governments to help decide whether to invest in a **major public project** such as a motorway or an airport. However, there is no reason in principle why a private sector investment, or indeed any action by a private economic agent or by the government, such as a tax change, cannot be examined by CBA.

CBA is an extension of the techniques of **investment appraisal** used by private sector firms to decide whether investment projects are commercially viable. Firms attempt to calculate all the private costs and benefits occurring in the *future* as a result of an investment or decision undertaken *now*. The central problem is guessing and putting money values to an unknown and uncertain future. But CBA is even more difficult because many of the social costs and benefits occurring in the future from an action undertaken now are externalities that are difficult to quantify. How does one put a monetary value on the saving of a human life resulting from fewer accidents on a proposed motorway? What is the social cost of the destruction of a beautiful view? It is extremely difficult to decide on all the likely costs and benefits, to draw the line on which to include and exclude, and to put monetary values on all the chosen costs and benefits accruing immediately and those that will only be received in the distant future.

Critics of CBA argue that it is pseudo-scientific — value judgements and arbitrary decisions disguised as objectivity. CBA is also criticised as a costly waste of time and money, and as a scam through which politicians distance themselves from, and induce delay in, unpopular decisions, deflecting the wrath of local communities on to supposedly impartial experts undertaking the CBA. Nevertheless, supporters of CBA argue that, for all its defects, it remains the best method of appraising public investment decisions because all the likely costs and benefits are exposed to public discussion.

### Government failure

There is a danger of assuming that market failure can be either reduced or completely eliminated, once identified, through appropriate government intervention: for example, by imposing taxes, controls and regulation. But there is another possibility: when the government intervenes to try to deal with a problem, far from curing or lessening the problem, intervention may make matters worse.

There are two very different approaches to the possibility of government failure, known respectively as the public interest and the public choice approach. In the **public interest** view, governments intervene benignly in the economy to eliminate waste and to achieve an efficient and socially desirable resource allocation. Markets fail and government intervention is necessary to correct market failure. **Public choice** theory, by contrast, argues that markets are more efficient than governments, whose intervention invariably produces an outcome inferior to that achieved by market forces. In the public choice view, we should be prepared to live with a degree of market failure rather than intervene in a well-intentioned but misguided way and end up creating worse problems.

## Examination questions and skills

Part (a) of EQ4 asks for an explanation of how attempts to correct market failures (other than negative externalities) may cause problems of government failure to replace those of market failure. Part (b) of the same question then asks for an assessment of the case for and against creating a market in tradable permits to pollute in order to reduce negative externalities associated with pollution. Part (d) of DRQ2 on the airline industry requires assessment of whether a cost–benefit analysis should be undertaken before a decision is made by the government on whether to build a third runway at London Heathrow airport.

As we have noted, the Module 1 specification requires candidates to acquire considerable knowledge of market failure, and to a lesser extent government failure, at AS. The A2 Module 5 specification for the most part then requires more advanced analysis and evaluation of the market failures covered in Module 1. You must use the concepts of allocative efficiency and inefficiency to explain why public goods, externalities and merit and demerit goods provide examples of market failure, and you must practise using diagrams that show private and social marginal costs and benefits to analyse market failures and possible policy responses.

## Common examination errors

Commonly made mistakes on market failure and government failure include the following:
- Failing to understand that market failure can be caused by both the inequitable and the inefficient functioning of markets.
- Showing a lack of awareness that monopoly and oligopoly can lead to market failure.
- Failing to apply correctly the concepts of allocative efficiency and inefficiency.
- Poorly drawn diagrams to show MPB, MSB, MPC and MSC.
- Wrongly asserting that government intervention always corrects market failure.
- Failing to appreciate the use and misuse of cost–benefit analysis.

# The labour market

These notes, which relate to AQA specification section 14.4, prepare you to answer AQA examination questions on:
- perfectly competitive labour markets
- imperfectly competitive or monopsonistic labour markets
- the effects of trade unions, the national minimum wage and discrimination in the labour market

## Essential information

### Applying price theory to the labour market

Labour market theory is really just the price theory that you have studied in the **goods market**, but operating in the **factor market**. Households and firms function simultaneously in both markets, but their roles are reversed. In the labour market, firms demand labour services that households supply.

### The supply of labour in a perfectly competitive labour market

The **market supply curve of labour** is obtained by adding together the **individual supply curves** of all the workers in the market. A worker's decision to supply one more hour of **labour time** must also mean that he or she sacrifices an hour of **leisure time**. For the worker to supply more labour, the hourly wage rate must rise to compensate for the fact that, as more money is earned, an extra pound means less and less, but an extra hour of leisure time sacrificed means more and more. (In economic terminology, the **marginal utility of money** falls and the **marginal utility of leisure time** rises as the worker supplies more labour, which eats into leisure time.) The resulting **upward-sloping supply curve of labour** is shown in Figure 21(a).

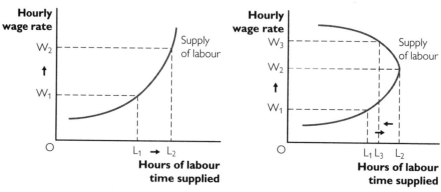

*(a) The upward–sloping supply curve of labour*

*(b) The backward-bending supply curve of labour*

*Figure 21 An individual's supply of labour*

At the going hourly wage rate, a worker will not wish to supply labour beyond the point at which **MU of the wage = MU of leisure**, other things remaining equal. At this content guidance

point, the wage received from the last hour worked yields the same utility as the last hour of leisure time enjoyed. To make it worthwhile for a worker to supply labour beyond this point, the hourly wage rate must rise: for example, from $W_1$ to $W_2$ in Figure 21(a). It is possible, however, that the supply curve may *bend backwards* above a certain wage rate ($W_2$ in Figure 21(b)), showing that as the wage rate rises above a critical level, the worker chooses to work fewer hours.

Whenever the hourly wage rate rises, an hour of leisure time becomes more expensive. Workers generally respond by working longer hours, thereby substituting more labour time in place of the now more expensive leisure time. This is the **substitution effect** of the rise in the wage rate. But an **income effect** also operates, which for some workers results in the **backward-bending supply curve of labour**. For most people, **leisure time is a normal good** and not an **inferior good**. A rise in the hourly wage rate increases the worker's real income, and as real income rises, so does demand for the normal good, leisure time. Above $W_2$ in Figure 21(b), this income effect of a wage rise becomes more powerful than the substitution effect. As a result, the worker chooses to work fewer hours so as to enjoy more leisure.

### The demand for labour in a perfectly competitive labour market
Firms demand labour because they believe profit can be made by selling the goods produced by their workers. This means that the demand for labour is a **derived demand**. Just as the market supply curve of labour in a perfectly competitive labour market is the sum of the supply curves of the individual workers in the labour market, so the **market demand curve for labour** is the sum of the demand curves for labour of each firm in the market. **Each firm's demand curve** is the **marginal revenue product (MRP)** of labour curve facing the firm in the labour market.

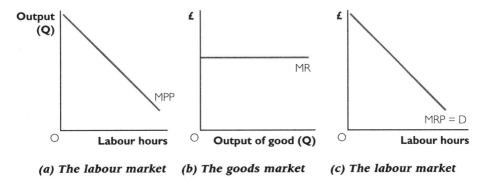

*(a) The labour market*    *(b) The goods market*    *(c) The labour market*

***Figure 22 Deriving a firm's demand curve for labour (the MRP curve) from the MPP curve***

The **marginal revenue product curve** shown in panel (c) of Figure 22 is obtained by multiplying the **marginal physical product (MPP) of labour** (shown in panel (a)) by **marginal revenue (MR)** (shown in panel (b)). The marginal physical product or MPP of labour is just another name for the **marginal returns** (or **marginal product**) of labour, which you first came across in the first topic, 'Firms, production and costs', pp. 15–20. Because of the **law of diminishing returns**, the marginal product of labour falls as additional workers are hired. As its name indicates, the MPP curve only shows the physical output produced by an extra worker — measured in whatever goods the firm produces. To convert this into a money value, the MPP of labour must be multiplied by marginal revenue. The end result is the MRP curve:

marginal revenue product = marginal physical product × marginal revenue

**The equilibrium wage and level of employment in a perfectly competitive labour market**

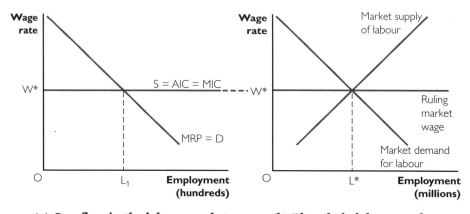

*(a) One firm in the labour market*     *(b) The whole labour market*

*Figure 23 The equilibrium wage rate and level of employment*

Having explained the supply curves of, and the demand curves for, labour, we are now in a position to show the determination of the **equilibrium wage rate** and **level of employment**, both for a single firm or employer within the market, and also for the whole labour market. These are shown respectively in panel (a) and panel (b) of Figure 23. The equilibrium wage rate W* and level of employment L* are determined in panel (b), where market demand equals market supply. Panel (a) then shows each firm as a price-taker at wage rate W*, which, as well as being the **perfectly elastic supply curve of labour** facing each firm, is also the **average input cost (AIC)** curve and the **marginal input cost (MIC) curve**. Because a firm can hire as many workers as it wants at W*, every time an extra worker is hired the firm's total wage bill rises by the wage paid to the new worker. Thus MIC equals the ruling wage, which is also the AIC (wage cost per worker).

To maximise profit when eventually selling the output produced by labour, the firm must demand labour up to the point at which:

the addition to sales revenue     =     the addition to production costs
from employing an extra worker          from employing an extra worker

or:

MRP = MIC

In a perfectly competitive labour market, MIC always equals the ruling wage, so the firm hires labour up to the point at which the **marginal revenue product of labour equals the wage rate (MRP = W)**. This is $L_1$ in Figure 23(a).

## Imperfectly competitive labour markets

A labour market in which there is a single employer is called a **monopsony**, and a market dominated by a single employer, but in which there are other employers, is **monopsonistic**. Monopsony means a single buyer, just as monopoly means a single seller. A monopsony is similar to a monopoly in many ways. As in monopoly, where consumers cannot choose between alternative suppliers of the good, in monopsony workers cannot choose between alternative employers. Only one firm or employer is available to hire their services. And in the same way that the market demand curve facing a monopoly supplier of a good is also the monopolist's average revenue curve, the market supply curve of labour is the monopsonist's average input cost (AIC) curve. The AIC curve shows the different wage rates that the monopsonist must pay to attract labour forces of different sizes. For example, Figure 24(a) shows a monopsony employer hiring ten workers at a weekly wage or AIC of £100 each. The diagram shows that with ten workers initially employed, the wage (or AIC) must rise from £100 to £110 a week to attract an eleventh worker.

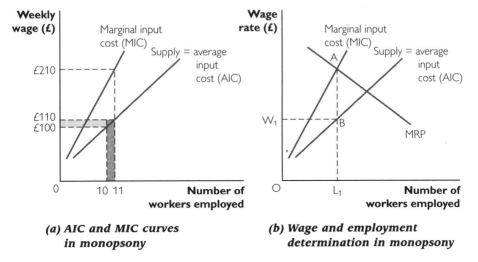

*(a) AIC and MIC curves in monopsony*

*(b) Wage and employment determination in monopsony*

*Figure 24 A monopsony labour market*

But in a monopsony labour market, the AIC curve is not the marginal input cost (MIC) curve of labour. To attract extra workers, the monopsonist must raise the weekly wage rate, paying the higher wage to all its workers. In this situation, the MIC incurred by employing an extra worker includes the total amount by which the wage bill rises, and not just the wage paid to the additional worker hired. The MIC curve is thus above the AIC or supply curve (just as in the goods market, a monopolist's MR curve is below its AR curve). In Figure 24(a), the MIC of employing the eleventh worker is £210 a week. This comprises the £110 paid to the eleventh worker (darker area in

Figure 24(a)), plus the £10 extra now paid to each of the original ten workers, which totals £100 (shown by the lighter shaded area in Figure 24(a)).

Figure 24(b) shows the equilibrium wage and level of employment in a monopsony labour market. As in a perfectly competitive labour market, the firm's equilibrium level of employment is determined where MRP = MIC. This is at point A in Figure 24(b). However, the equilibrium wage is *below* A and *less* than the MRP of labour, being determined at point B on the supply curve of labour. Although the monopsonist *could* pay a wage determined at A and equal to the MRP of labour, without incurring a loss on the last worker employed, it has no need to. The monopsonist can employ all the workers it requires by paying the wage $W_1$, determined at point B.

## Trade unions and labour markets

A **trade union** is an association of workers formed to protect and promote the interests of its members. A union's main function is to bargain with employers to improve wages and other conditions of work. Acting as a monopoly supplier of labour, a union may try to set the wage rate above the market-clearing wage rate, leaving employment to be determined by the amount of labour that employers hire at the wage set by the union. Figure 25(a) shows the effect of a union setting the wage rate above the market-clearing rate in a (previously) perfectly competitive labour market. Employment falls from $L_1$ to $L_2$.

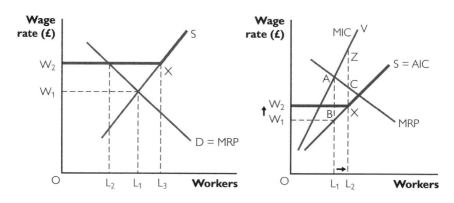

*(a) A union–set wage in a competitive labour market*

*(b) A union–set wage in a monopsony labour market*

**Figure 25 The effect of introducing a trade union into competitive and monopsony labour markets**

But in the monopsony labour market shown in Figure 25(b), a union may be able to raise *both* the wage rate and employment. In the absence of a union, the employment level is $L_1$, determined at point A where MRP = MIC, and the wage rate is $W_1$, determined at point B. If the union sets the wage rate at $W_2$, the 'kinked' line $W_2$XS becomes the labour supply curve (and also the AIC curve) facing the monopsonist employer. However, at wage rate $W_2$, the monopsonist's MIC curve is the 'double kinked' line $W_2$XZV. Employment rises to $L_2$, the level of employment at which the MRP curve intersects the vertical section between X and Z at point C on the 'double-kinked' MIC curve. Both the wage rate and employment have risen compared to the situation without a union.

## The effect of a national minimum wage

Figure 25 can also be used to explain and analyse the possible effects of introducing a **national minimum wage rate**. In a competitive labour market, a minimum wage rate set at $W_2$ increases wages for workers who keep their jobs, but creates unemployment. By contrast, both wages *and* employment may rise if the labour market is monopsonistic.

## The theory of wage discrimination

Just as *price discrimination* occurs when firms with *monopoly* power charge different prices based on customers' different willingness to pay, so **wage discrimination** takes place when employers with *monopsony* power pay **different wages based on workers' different willingness to supply labour**. In the absence of wage discrimination, all workers in a competitive labour market (shown in Figure 26) receive a wage rate of $W_1$, determined by supply and demand. Employers' total wage costs are shown by the rectangle $OW_1AL_1$. But if, instead of paying $W_1$ to all workers, employers pay each worker the minimum he or she is prepared to work for, the total wage bill falls to equal the shaded 'wedge' area $OBAL_1$. Employers thus gain at the expense of workers, which is why firms pay, and trade unions resist, discriminatory wages whenever possible.

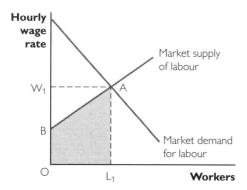

*Figure 26 Wage discrimination*

## Other explanations of different wages

Even in highly competitive labour markets, wage differences exist, largely because the labour demand and supply curves are in different positions in different labour markets, reflecting factors such as varying labour productivity, ability and required skill. Also, different jobs have **different non-monetary characteristics**, often in the form of **job satisfaction** or **dissatisfaction**. Other things being equal, a worker must be paid a higher wage to compensate for any relative unpleasantness in the job. An **equalising wage differential** is the payment that must be made to compensate a worker for the different non-monetary characteristics of jobs so that, following the payment, the worker has no incentive to switch between jobs or labour markets.

Different wages paid to different groups of workers may also result from forms of **labour market discrimination** unrelated to the theory of wage discrimination. Some **employers discriminate on the basis of race, religion, gender and age**, even though such discrimination is usually illegal. Workers suffering labour market discrimination have poorer job opportunities and are generally less well paid than workers fortunate enough to avoid such discrimination.

## Examination questions and skills

Part (a) of EQ5 asks why some workers are paid more than others, while part (b) asks for an evaluation of whether trade unions can only increase wages for their members at the expense of reduced levels of employment.

Essay questions in the examination are likely to ask for explanation, analysis and evaluation of the functioning of different labour markets (perfectly competitive and/or oligopolistic), whereas data-response questions might home in on particular real-world labour markets and require the application of the theoretical concepts explained in these notes to the issues posed by the question.

## Common examination errors

Commonly made mistakes on the labour market include the following:
- Failing to understand the reversal of roles of households and firms in the labour market, with firms exercising demand for labour and households exercising supply.
- Failing to appreciate that maximising principles (profit for firms and utility for workers) underlie labour market theory.
- Writing about the whole market when the question asks for analysis of one firm within the market, and vice versa.
- Inaccurate analysis of the demand for labour in terms of marginal productivity theory.
- Lack of understanding of monopsonistic labour markets.
- Writing 'commonsense' superficial accounts of wage differences without using labour market theory.

# Income, wealth and poverty

These notes, which relate to AQA specification sections 14.4 and 14.5, prepare you to answer AQA examination questions on:
- the distribution of income and wealth
- notions of equity
- the problem of poverty
- government policies to alleviate poverty and influence the distribution of income and wealth

# Essential information

## Income and wealth

Income and wealth illustrate the key difference between flow and stock concepts in economics. **Income** is a **flow**, measured per period of time: for example, weekly, monthly and annually. The **stock** of **wealth**, by contrast, accumulates over time. The different **factors of production** receive different types of income. **Employees** are paid **wages** and **salaries**; **owners of land and property** receive **rent**; **interest** is paid to **lenders of financial capital**; and **profit** is the **residual** earned by the **owners of businesses** and **entrepreneurs**. **Transfers**, such as unemployment benefits, are another very important type of income, especially for the poor. As the name indicates, transfers shift income from taxpayers to benefit recipients, without production of a good or service by the person receiving the benefit. Income can also be classified as **total original income, gross income** and **disposable income**. These terms are defined in Table 1.

*Table 1 Distribution of income in the UK, 1999/2000*
*(quintile groups of households, £ per year)*

|  | Total original income Income before tax and receiving welfare benefits | Gross income Original income plus welfare benefits | Disposable income Gross income less income tax, national insurance contributions and local taxes |
|---|---|---|---|
| Top 20% | 54,400 | 55,540 | 42,450 |
| Next 20% | 27,920 | 30,040 | 23,640 |
| Middle 20% | 17,170 | 21,010 | 17,210 |
| Next 20% | 7,680 | 12,810 | 11,000 |
| Bottom 20% | 2,840 | 7,720 | 6,830 |
| All households | 22,000 | 25,420 | 20,230 |

Source: *Social Trends* 32, 2002.

People can hold wealth in **physical assets** such as land, houses, art and antiques, or in **financial assets** such as stocks and shares. Houses and shares are forms of **marketable wealth**, whose value can **appreciate** (go up in value) or **depreciate** (go down in value). Some forms of wealth are **non-marketable**: for example, the stock of wealth accumulated when a person contributes to a pension scheme cannot be sold to someone else.

## Inequalities in the distribution of income and wealth

In the UK, as in most other countries, the **distributions of income and wealth are both unequal**, but — as Tables 1 and 2 show — **the distribution of wealth is significantly more unequal than the distribution of income**. The link between wealth and income partly explains this. For the better-off, wealth generates investment income, part of which — being saved — then adds to wealth and generates even more income. The poor, by contrast, who possess little or no wealth, also have incomes (from low-paid jobs and/or welfare benefits) that are too low to allow saving and the accumulation of wealth. The tax system also provides an explanation. In the UK income is usually taxed, but wealth is generally untaxed (except through **inheritance tax** and **capital gains tax**).

*Table 2 Distribution of wealth in the UK, 1999*

| Percentage of wealth owned by: | |
|---|---|
| Wealthiest 1% | 23% |
| Wealthiest 5% | 43% |
| Wealthiest 10% | 54% |
| Wealthiest 25% | 74% |
| Wealthiest 50% | 94% |

Source: *Social Trends* 32, 2002.

### The measurement of inequalities in the distribution of income

The extent to which the distribution of income is equal or unequal can be illustrated on **Lorenz curve** diagrams, such as that drawn in Figure 27, with the degree of inequality measured by a statistic known as a **Gini coefficient**.

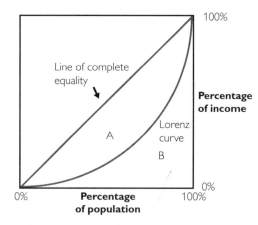

*Figure 27 The Lorenz curve*

The Lorenz curve in Figure 27 shows population on the horizontal axis, measured in cumulative percentages from 0 to 100%. The vertical axes shows the cumulative percentage of income received by the population. If incomes were distributed equally, the Lorenz curve would lie along the diagonal line. The nearer the Lorenz curve is to the diagonal, the more equal is the distribution of income. The Gini coefficient measures the area between the Lorenz curve and the diagonal as a ratio of the total area under the diagonal.

In Figure 27 the Gini coefficient is calculated using the following formula:

$$\text{Gini coefficient} = \frac{\text{area A}}{\text{area A + area B}}$$

## Reasons for an unequal distribution of income

The **labour market theory** covered in the previous topic, 'The labour market' (pp. 52–58), provides part of the explanation for income inequalities. **Different supply and demand conditions** (including differing **labour productivity**) in different labour markets lead to different equilibrium wages, while employers' **monopsony power** and an **absence of countervailing union power** might drive down wages in particular labour markets. However, the lowest incomes are received by the **unwaged** rather than by the **low-waged**. The **unemployed** and **elderly people** who are solely reliant on the **state old age pension** are two of the groups with the lowest incomes.

In part, the growing *relative* inequality of the unemployed and the elderly has been caused by the way welfare benefits are adjusted each year. Before the early 1980s, unemployment benefit, the state pension and other welfare benefits increased each year in line with changes in the **index of average earnings**, so the unwaged shared in increasing national prosperity. As average earnings generally rise faster than inflation, the **real income** of benefit recipients increased by the same amount as the average of people in work. But since the early 1980s, welfare benefits have been **index linked** to the **retail price index (RPI)**, which generally rises by less than the index of average earnings. As a result, inequality between people with jobs and those without jobs has grown.

## Inequality, market failure and government failure

Unregulated market forces tend to produce highly unequal distributions of income and wealth, which many economists deem **inequitable, unjust** or **unfair**. They argue that government intervention, usually through **progressive taxation** (taxing the rich more proportionately than the poor) and **transfers** from rich to poor, should be used to reduce inequalities. But free-market economists generally believe that such intervention, although well intentioned, results in problems of **government failure** that are worse than the supposed **market failure** that intervention aims to correct. They argue that, if taxes are too progressive and benefits too generous, **labour market incentives** are destroyed. The economy becomes less competitive, economic growth stalls, and the poor end up being *absolutely* worse off than they would have been had growth been faster, even though *relative* to the rich, the poor are better off. The poor would benefit more, they argue, from greater inequality, faster growth and the **'trickle-down' effect** that might occur as the rich spend their wealth and high incomes on goods and services produced by the poor.

So what has actually happened in the UK? During much of the twentieth century, progressive taxation and transfers reduced income inequalities, except during the 1980s and 1990s when free-market **supply-side policies** widened inequalities. At the beginning of the twenty-first century, government policy has once again had some success in reducing income inequality, though whether this has harmed growth is debatable.

## Horizontal and vertical equity

**Equity**, which means fairness or justness, is a **normative** concept (a matter of opinion), whereas the closely related, but not identical, concept of **equality** can be measured and is therefore a **positive** concept. Government intervention in the economy, which treats people *in the same circumstances* equally, obeys the principle of **horizontal equity**. For example, horizontal equity occurs when households with the same income and personal circumstances (for example, the same number of children) pay the same income tax and are eligible for the same welfare benefits.

**Vertical equity** is much more controversial, since it justifies taking income from the rich (on the grounds that they do not need it) and redistributing their income to the poor (on the grounds that they do need it). The distribution of income after taxation and receipt of transfers is judged more equitable. Achieving greater vertical equity can conflict with another principle of intervention, the **benefit principle**, which argues that those who receive most benefit from government spending (such as motorists benefiting from roads) should pay the most in taxes.

### Poverty

Poverty is obviously very closely related to inequalities in the distribution of income and wealth. However, we must distinguish between *absolute* poverty and *relative* poverty. Because the UK is a high-income developed economy, in which welfare benefits provide a minimum income and 'safety net' for the poor, very few people are absolutely poor in the sense that poor people in less economically developed countries are. For the most part, the problem of poverty in the UK is one of relative poverty. A household is in **relative poverty** if its income is below a specified proportion of average income for all households: for example, less than a third of average income. Possible causes of relative poverty include: unemployment, especially long-term unemployment; old age and longevity; single parenthood; the decline of employment opportunities in traditional industries and skill fields; lack of education and training; the fall in the value of welfare and unemployment benefits relative to wages and salaries; and the higher incomes and tax cuts enjoyed by the better-off.

By contrast, **absolute poverty** occurs when income is below a particular specified level. When *all* incomes grow, *absolute* poverty falls, but *relative* poverty falls only if low incomes grow at a faster rate than average incomes.

### Government policies to reduce poverty

By reducing inequalities in the distribution of income, progressive taxation and trans-fers (welfare benefits) can reduce absolute and relative poverty — providing labour market incentives, competitiveness and economic growth do not worsen significantly. All economists agree, however, that *absolute* poverty, though not necessarily *relative* poverty, can best be reduced by fast and sustained economic growth and by creating jobs. As noted earlier, very low incomes generally result from being *unwaged* rather than *low-waged*.

### The poverty trap or earnings trap

In so far as low-waged workers are poor, their ability to escape from poverty may be limited by the existence of the **poverty trap** (or **earnings trap**). The immediate cause of the poverty trap is the overlap — which is illustrated in Figure 28 — between the **income tax threshold** (the level of income at which income tax starts to be paid) and the **means-tested welfare benefits ceiling** (the level of income at which means-tested transfer incomes cease to be paid). When welfare benefits are means-tested, a person's right to claim the benefit is reduced and eventually disappears completely, as income rises. A low-paid worker caught within this zone of overlap not only pays **income tax** and **national insurance contributions (NICs)** on each extra pound earned; he or she also loses part or all of the right to claim benefits. Thus low-paid workers and their families whose income falls within this zone of overlap have become trapped in relative poverty, since any increase in their pay results in little or no increase — and in extreme cases, in a fall — in their disposable income. The effective **marginal rate of taxation** of workers in poorly paid occupations is therefore very high indeed when the loss of means-tested benefits is added to deductions through income tax and NICs.

The poverty trap could be eliminated by getting rid of the zone of overlap in the **income pyramid** illustrated in Figure 28. The income tax threshold could be raised to take low-waged households out of the tax net. Means-tested benefits could be replaced by **universal benefits** (benefits claimable as of right, and unrelated to income). But as taxes would have to increase to pay for any substantial increase in universal benefits, the poor might end up more heavily taxed! By preventing employers paying 'poverty wages', the **national minimum wage** may also reduce both poverty and the poverty trap, though this could also be counterproductive if unemployment increases as a result.

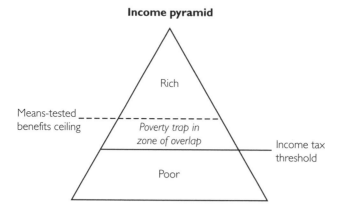

**Figure 28 The poverty trap**

## Examination questions and skills

Part (a) of DRQ4 asks for a comparison of recent changes in the relative importance of spending on different welfare benefits. Parts (b), (c) and (d) respectively test understanding of the index-linking of welfare benefits, analysis of how means-tested and universal benefits affect supply-side incentives, and evaluation of policies to reduce or eliminate the poverty trap. Part (c) of DRQ3 asks for analysis of how the changing nature of the family has affected the distribution of income in the UK.

Examination questions are likely to ask for description of inequalities in the distributions of income and/or wealth, explanation and analysis of the causes of identified inequalities, assessment of the implications of inequality for the UK economy and/or evaluation of policies that governments use or might use to reduce inequality.

## Common examination errors

Commonly made mistakes on income, wealth and poverty include the following:

- Confusing income as a *flow* with wealth as a *stock*.
- Inability to explain and analyse inequalities and poverty in terms of market failure and government failure.
- Confusing equity with equality.
- Lack of understanding of how progressive taxes and transfers can, in principle, reduce inequality.
- Failing to apply supply and demand analysis and labour market theory to explain income inequality.
- Confusing absolute poverty and relative poverty.
- Lack of awareness of poverty traps other than the earnings trap: for example, to get a job a person may need a home, but to get a home a person may need a job.

# Questions
# &
# Answers

This section includes 9 examination-style questions designed to be a key learning, revision and exam preparation resource. There are four data-response questions (DRQs) and five essay questions (EQs). The four DRQs are similar in layout, structure and style to the compulsory question in Section A of the Unit 5 examination. Each question can be used as part of a trial or mock exam near the end of your course. Alternatively, as you study a topic in the Content Guidance section of this guide, you could refer selectively to particular sub-parts of each question, as indicated in the 'Examination questions and skills' advice at the end of each topic.

Likewise, you can use the EQs in this section either as timed test questions in the lead-up to the examination or to reinforce your understanding of the specification subject matter, topic by topic, as you proceed through the Content Guidance. The EQs are similar to the three questions from which you must choose one in Section B of the Unit 5 examination.

This section also includes:
- A student's answer of grade A to D standard for each DRQ and EQ.
- Examiner's comments on each student's answer, explaining — where relevant — how the answer could be improved and a higher grade or mark achieved. These comments are denoted by the symbol 🄮.

**Note:** It is important to understand the difference between two types of marks that GCE examining boards award for candidates' work: **raw marks** and **uniform standardised marks (USMs)**.

Raw marks are the marks awarded out of 50 (for each DRQ and EQ) by the examiner who reads your script. After all the grade boundaries have been set as raw marks, each candidate's raw mark for the Unit 5 paper is converted into a USM. Uniform standardised marks have the same grade boundaries — for all subjects and all unit exams. These are: grade A: 80%; grade B: 70%; grade C: 60%; grade D: 50%; grade E: 40%.

The marks awarded for students' answers to each DRQ and EQ in the following pages are raw marks and not USMs. A likely grade is indicated at the end of each student's answer, based on the qualities shown in each part of the answer. It must be stressed that the actual raw mark at which a particular grade boundary is set varies from examination to examination, depending on factors such as whether the questions have turned out to be relatively easy or relatively difficult, when compared to questions in previous examinations.

# Data-response questions
## Question 1
### The computer games market

**Total for this question: 50 marks**

Study **Extracts A** and **B**, and answer **all** parts of the question that follows.

**Extract A: The fight for dominance in the computer games industry**

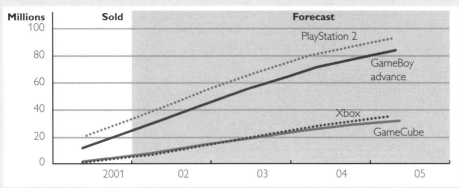

Source: *Independent*, 7 June 2002.

*Estimated cumulative sales of consoles, 2001–05*

The battle for supremacy in the console market has been fought over four rounds, with the fifth round now being fought and decided. Each round has been based on a particular level of technology and has had a clear winner, because software developers write games for the most popular machine, and consumers buy the machine with the best software and choice of games. 5

**Round 1 Atari:** In the late 1970s and early 1980s, Atari, an American company with a Japanese name, dominated and Space Invaders was the rage.

**Round 2 Nintendo:** Thanks to a gorilla called Donkey Kong and a moustachioed Italian plumber called Mario, Atari was overthrown by Nintendo.

**Round 3 Sega:** But soon the technology changed again. Sega entered the market with 10 a more powerful console, the Megadrive. By 1992, Super Mario was playing second fiddle to a new cartoon character, Sonic the Hedgehog.

**Round 4 Sony:** The 1995 arrival of PlayStation 1 rolled over everything in its path. This was a great machine, but not noticeably better than its competitors. The main differences were in Sony's strategy and marketing. 15

# data-response question 1

**Round 5 PlayStation 2 versus Xbox versus GameCube:** Sony's PlayStation 2 looks like being the winner. In an aggressive price war, Sony, Microsoft and Nintendo have all slashed console prices below cost, hoping to cross-subsidise losses from the fat profit margins made from the royalties charged to developers and manufacturers of the games played on their machines.

20

Source: adapted from articles in the *Independent*, 7 June 2002, and the *Guardian*, 14 March 1998 and 14 October 1999.

### Extract B: Should the prices charged for computer games be regulated?

The prices charged for computed games are artificially high because of insufficient competition. In the UK games are roughly 30 per cent more expensive than in the USA. This is partly because retailers' margins and indirect taxes are higher in Britain. But it is also possible that Sony and Nintendo are charging higher wholesale prices than in the USA. They may be segmenting the market in order to discriminate on prices.

5

But even if the computer games industry operates against the public interest, it is difficult to decide what to do. One option is to impose price controls. A second option is to attack the licensing arrangements which enable the console manufacturers to extend their dominance in hardware to software. A final option is to do nothing and allow market forces and technical advances to undermine the incumbent firms' dominance.

10

Source: adapted from an article in the *Financial Times*, 17 January 1994.

(a) Using information from the data, describe the structure of the computer games industry. (4 marks)

(b) Lines 17–20 of Extract A state that manufacturers are often prepared to sell games consoles at a loss. Explain why this is so. (6 marks)

(c) Lines 2–6 of Extract B suggest that by charging higher prices in the UK than in the USA, games companies may be price discriminating. With the help of appropriate diagrams, analyse how such price discrimination takes place. (10 marks)

(d) Evaluate the three policy options outlined in Extract B for trying to ensure that the prices charged by computer games companies are in the public interest. (30 marks)

■ ■ ■

## Candidate's answer

**(a)** The computer games industry divides into firms which manufacture games consoles or hardware, and those that manufacture games or software. As Extract A shows, there are now three main hardware companies, Sony, Nintendo and Microsoft, though other companies have been important in the past, e.g. Atari and Sega.

✎ This is a poor answer that just scrapes 1 of the 4 marks available (for mentioning the division between the hardware and software parts of the computer games industry). The candidate also obeys the instruction to use information from the data, but unfortunately the answer lacks any mention of the technical terms expected at A-level, such as imperfect competition, competitive oligopoly and market concentration. **1/4 marks**

**(b)** When shops sell goods below cost and at a loss, it is called loss-leading. By advertising special offers in their windows, the shops attract customers inside, who then spend money on other goods at the full price.

✎ The candidate has identified a possible reason (loss leading) for selling games consoles at a loss, but because he does not make any specific and relevant reference to games consoles, the answer can only earn 2 marks. To earn more marks, he might explain that the greater the number of consumers owning, say, a PlayStation 2, the greater the number also of PlayStation 2 games that will be sold. The hardware manufacturers earn royalty payments from each game sold for their consoles. Using technical jargon, the console manufacturers are willing to cross-subsidise losses incurred by selling the hardware below cost, from the profits made on the software. The manufacturers are also willing to sell hardware below cost, or at a very low profit margin, in order to establish a network of millions of users worldwide who, having bought a PlayStation 2 (for example), are then 'locked in' to the machine. **2/6 marks**

**(c)** The diagrams I have drawn below illustrate how games companies may be charging discriminatory prices.

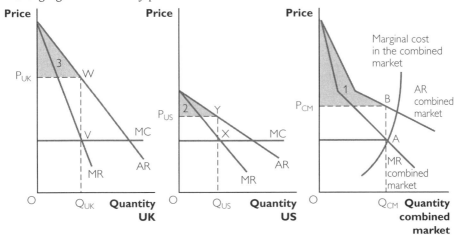

The right-hand diagram shows what happens in the combined US and UK markets if games companies charge the same (profit-maximising) price to all customers, irrespective of which country they live in. The profit-maximising output $Q_{CM}$ is determined at point A where MR = MC, and the price charged is $P_{CM}$. Consumer welfare (or consumer surplus) is shown by the shaded area 1.

I shall now explain what happens if a games company charges discriminatory prices. First, the company must identify different markets, in this case the UK and US markets, with different elasticities of demand. The left-hand diagram shows that at all prices, demand in the UK is more inelastic than demand in the USA (shown in the centre diagram). Price discrimination occurs when different prices are charged in different sub-markets, based on customers' different willingness to pay rather than on any difference in costs of production. UK customers are willing to pay more, so they are charged more ($P_{UK}$). American customers are charged the lower price of $P_{US}$. Successful price discrimination enables the games companies to boost profits by taking consumer surplus away from consumers. Following successful price discrimination, consumer surplus falls to area 2 (in the US market) and area 3 (in the UK market). The combined area 2 plus 3 is less than area 1 in the right-hand panel, which, as I said earlier, depicts consumer surplus when there is no price discrimination.

> 🖉 The candidate earns full marks for this question. His diagram is excellent, though he could have saved valuable exam time (given that this is only a 10-mark question) by omitting the right-hand panel of the diagram and restricting his analysis to the left-hand and centre panels. His analysis of consumer surplus, while accurate and providing an excellent application of an important concept, is not strictly relevant to this question. By omitting this analysis, he would have freed time to explain how, in order to maximise profit over both sub-markets, the games company must produce where MR = MC in each sub-market (at point X in the US market and point V in the UK market). The price charged is then determined respectively at points Y and W, on the relevant demand (or AR) curve immediately above X and V. Also, he might have noted that successful price discrimination requires not only the identification of different customers with different elasticities of demand, but the prevention of seepage. Seepage occurs if US customers, buying at the cheaper American price, resell to British customers, thereby undercutting the games company's UK price, or if Britons travel to the USA to buy their games at the lower US price. Different technical specifications for consoles and games in the USA and the UK can prevent such seepage. **10/10 marks**

**(d)** The three policy options mentioned in Extract B are (i) imposing price controls; (ii) making licensing arrangements illegal; and (iii) doing nothing and leaving the market to find a solution. I shall consider each of these in turn.

(i) Imposing price controls. Price controls are an example of what economists call 'command and control' regulation. The rationale for price controls is that the games companies are exploiting their monopoly power, restricting output and raising prices above marginal cost. Whenever P > MC, allocative inefficiency results. By trying to set the price control so that P = MC, the policy-makers are trying to improve allocative efficiency.

This is fine in theory, but there is no guarantee that the price control will be set at the allocatively efficient level. If a price ceiling is imposed below the market-clearing price, excess demand will result. Queues, waiting lists and black markets may result, and to some extent, who ends up successfully buying a computer game or console may depend on pot luck.

(ii) Making licensing arrangements illegal. The snag is that licensing arrangements are often global, so action by the UK alone could only have a limited impact. Many software suppliers might not wish to compete aggressively with console manufacturers in Britain if they were still tied to them in other markets.

(iii) Doing nothing and leaving the market to find a solution. At first sight, this might appear to be the worst of the three possible solutions, since it smacks of just allowing firms with monopoly power to continue to exploit their customers. But there is what I consider to be a very strong argument in favour of this option. Seventy years ago, Joseph Schumpeter developed the theory of 'creative destruction' in monopoly. Schumpeter argued that many monopolies are virtuous rather than malign, because their monopoly position and power result from being better than their competitors. They are more innovative and dynamically efficient. But once their power is established, it is difficult to stay ahead of the game. New products are developed and technologies change, until eventually the monopoly power of firms that had once seemed invincible is either destroyed or becomes irrelevant. IBM and Microsoft provide a very good example. In the 1980s (before Microsoft was formed), many people believed that IBM's monopoly power was dangerous. But technical change in ICT-related industries reduced IBM to one player among many. Today, many people argue that Microsoft's monopoly power is also dangerous. My view is that the market will sort Microsoft out; eventually new technologies and competitors will emerge.

Returning to the computer games market, Extract A provides evidence to support my argument. Once-dominant companies such as Atari and Sega have disappeared into oblivion. The same might happen to Sony and Microsoft without the need for governments to impose price controls or to regulate. I rest my case.

This is an excellent answer that reaches Level 5. The answer lacks an explicit conclusion, but because of the quality of his answer, the candidate successfully picks up marks for the skill of evaluation from all his main points. However, if time permits, it is always best to write a conclusion firmly stating (in this case) which option is best and why. Had the candidate argued against leaving it for the market to sort out, he might conclude that as both policy options have merits and demerits, the use of price controls and making licensing arrangements illegal should best be regarded as complementary policies rather than as substitutes. A conclusion that 'it all depends' can be quite a good strategy — provided sufficient justification is given.

**28/30 marks**

**Scored 41/50    82% = grade A**

# ata-response question 2

# Question 2
## Budget or low-cost airlines

**Total for this question: 50 marks**

Study **Extracts A, B** and **C**, and answer **all** parts of the question that follows.

**Extract A: Variable costs incurred by selected European airlines and average flight length**

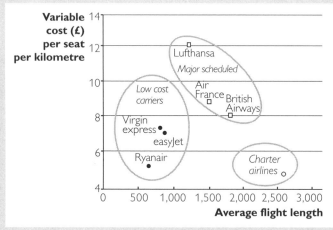

Source: *Financial Times*, 7 May 2002.

**Extract B: Two rival business models for low-cost airline**

easyJet's takeover of Go has thrown into sharp relief two different business models for Europe's budget airlines. Only one of them can win. There are now two big budget airlines in Europe, the expanded easyJet and Ryanair. Both are fast growing and profitable and both use highly variable pricing, reflecting demand for their flights. Both try to keep the marginal cost of passenger journeys as low as possible. 5

But there is an important difference. easyJet is in more direct competition with the established larger airlines. The airline flies to more established airports and the flights are designed to appeal as much to budget-conscious business travellers as to leisure passengers. Ryanair emphasises prices that are low in *absolute* terms, in order to compete with alternative uses of time and money. EasyJet's is certainly not a high- 10 price strategy but its emphasis is on prices that are lower than the big airlines in *relative* terms.

easyJet's approach is the riskier because it relies on defeating the large airlines in their heartland rather than on carving out a protected area at the bottom of the market

as Ryanair has done. Eventually easyJet may be squeezed between the lowest-cost    15
competitor, Ryanair, and the large airlines that have learnt how to compete with it.
They will do this in a number of ways: partly through cost-cutting; partly through
aggressive price cutting on vulnerable routes cross-subsidised by profits made on
routes where there is less competition; partly through a form of regulatory capture
which might make it hard for easyJet to gain access to landing slots at key airports;    20
and partly because easyJet's increasing size will bring not economies of scale but the
burdens of complexity too. As it starts to look more like the big airlines, easyJet will
acquire some of their costs too.

Source: adapted from an article in the *Financial Times* by Peter Martin, 7 May 2002.

### Extract C: A threefold increase in air travel predicted by 2020

A recent report has predicted a 300% growth in air travel over the next 20 years. To
meet this growth in demand, a third runway at Heathrow airport has been proposed
to allow an extra 500 flights a day over London. The report estimates that only 260
homes will have to be knocked down to make way for the runway. But the report also
warns that 35,000 people are at risk from nitrogen dioxide pollution that causes lung    5
disease and breathing problems. More than 10,000 homes might have to be pulled
down. The local MP says: 'Nobody believes that only 260 homes will go. Many more
properties will be lost because of the noise and pollution.'

Source: adapted from articles in the *Independent*, 31 July 2002,
and the *Daily Mail*, 3 August 2002.

(a) **Briefly state two reasons why the variable costs of the budget airlines shown
in Extract A are lower than those of the major scheduled airlines.** (4 marks)

(b) **Line 5 of Extract B states that both Ryanair and easyJet 'try to keep the
marginal cost of passenger journeys as low as possible'. What is marginal cost,
and how may the marginal cost of a passenger journey affect an airline's profit?** (6 marks)

(c) **Analyse two of the ways indicated in lines 17–22 of Extract B through which
the large airlines could compete against easyJet.** (10 marks)

(d) **Assess the view that a cost–benefit analysis should be undertaken before the
government decides whether to build a third runway at London Heathrow
airport.** (30 marks)

■ ■ ■

## Candidate's answer

(a) An airline's fixed costs include the cost of fuel used by its aircraft. Two reasons
why a budget airline such as easyJet incurs lower variable costs than a major
schedule airline such as British Airways are (i) the budget airlines operate from
less fashionable airports that charge a lower landing fee per flight; and (ii) the

costs per passenger per flight are less because passengers have to pay for food and drink in cash on the flight as easyJet does not provide them free.

> 🖉 This answer earns full marks, giving two accurate reasons why the variable costs of budget airlines are lower than those of the major airlines. **4/4 marks**

**(b)** Marginal cost is the extra cost incurred when, in this case, an airline carries one extra passenger on its aircraft. If marginal cost (MC) is *below* marginal revenue (MR), the airline's profit will increase when one more passenger buys a flight ticket. Conversely, if MC is *above* MR, an extra passenger adds more to the airline's costs than he does to total sales revenue, thus reducing the airline's total profit.

> 🖉 The answer is completely accurate, but doesn't quite earn full marks. To gain the extra mark, the candidate needs to relate marginal cost to a budget airline such as easyJet or Ryanair. She could do this by explaining that, when a ticket is sold to an extra passenger on an aircraft with plenty of empty (unsold) seats, the marginal cost incurred by the airline is close to zero. The seat will fly to the aircraft's destination whether or not a passenger uses it. The marginal cost of supply of an otherwise empty seat is largely restricted to ticket sale cost and the cost of any extra fuel used by the aircraft. Provided the passenger buys the ticket at a price above this very low marginal cost of supply, the sale adds to the airline's profit. **5/6 marks**

**(c)** The two ways mentioned in Extract B through which the large airlines could compete against easyJet which I shall analyse are: (i) 'through aggressive price-cutting on vulnerable routes cross-subsidised by profits made on routes where there is less competition'; and (ii) through regulatory capture.

Suppose easyJet starts to operate a cut-price service on the London to Moscow route, which is already served by a British Airways standard fare scheduled flight. BA might (subject to the competition authorities in Britain and Europe not intervening) indulge in *predatory pricing*, i.e. BA might reduce ticket prices below cost and subsidise the resulting loss on the London to Moscow route with profit made on BA's many other routes where ticket prices have not been cut. Once having 'killed off' easyJet on this route, BA would restore prices to their previous level.

Regulatory capture occurs when regulators appointed by governments to protect consumers' interests 'go native' and start to side with the companies they are supposed to regulate. Large airlines might indulge in a form of regulatory capture by successfully persuading the regulators to withhold licences they might otherwise grant to budget airlines to fly on routes already operated by the big airlines. In effect, the regulator creates an artificial barrier to entry, which protects the monopoly position of the big airlines and prevents or reduces market contestability.

> 🖉 This is an excellent answer, which is extremely well focused and to the point. The candidate obeys the instruction to analyse, and it is difficult to see how this answer could be improved. **10/10 marks**

**(d)** Cost–benefit analysis (CBA) tries to identify all the costs and benefits of a major investment project such as a third runway at Heathrow airport, placing monetary values on each cost and benefit, and then coming to a conclusion as to whether the project is in the public interest on the ground that the benefits must exceed the costs. I am going to question whether CBA can calculate correctly *all* the costs and benefits of the project and correctly place monetary values on them. Then, I am going to conclude whether, in the light of my answer to the first question, the government should spend taxpayers' money on CBA.

A third runway at Heathrow airport will have a life extending scores of years into the future, maybe even centuries. How far into the future should the CBA go, before deciding when to exclude and stop measuring costs and benefits occurring beyond the 'cut-off' date? And how should CBA value future costs and benefits in comparison with current costs and benefits? CBA generally values future costs and benefits less than current costs and benefits (i.e. it *discounts* the value of future costs and benefits, with the amount of the *discount* being greater, the further into the future we go).

A second major problem stems from the fact that *social* cost–benefit analysis estimates the values of the external benefits (positive externalities) and external costs (negative externalities) resulting from the investment project, as well as the private costs and benefits of the airport and airlines using the airport. Which externalities should be included in the CBA, and how should they be valued? CBA places monetary values on externalities which, by their nature, are not easily quantifiable, as there is no market in an externality in which market price could quantify the value of the externality. How should the destruction of an ancient church to make way for the runway be valued? How should the extra noise and atmospheric pollution that use of the runway may generate be valued? In a CBA undertaken to decide the location of a third London airport, choice of location hinged on how an hour of a businessman's time is valued. A high value placed on an hour of a businessman's time travelling between central London and the airport favoured a location close to central London, whereas a lower value would have justified a location further away.

This brings me to my second question: should the government spend taxpayers' money on a CBA? The case against centres on the argument that CBA is expensive and unreliable because it depends on arbitrary judgements on how to answer the questions I posed earlier. Also the time taken to undertake a CBA induces unnecessary delay in the completion of a project that might be vital for the UK economy. If Britain does not expand Heathrow, vital business might be lost to Paris, Frankfurt and Amsterdam, which have no qualms about expanding their airports speedily. So in conclusion, I believe these arguments suggest a conclusion that the runway is in the public interest on the grounds that the benefits exceed the costs, but there is a danger that CBA will waste resources and induce unnecessary delay into decision making.

# data-response question 2

This is a very good answer in many respects, but, because of a couple of omissions, I have placed it near the top of Level 4 (18–24 marks), rather than in Level 5. The first omission is a lack of explanation and analysis of externalities. The answer would have benefited from at least one marginal private and social costs and benefits diagram, with accompanying explanation related to the proposed runway. Second, 'evaluation marks' are lost because the candidate explains, clearly and quite fully, the disadvantages of CBA, but does not explain any advantages (such as consideration of externalities, transparency in decision making and the government seeking the advice of supposedly independent experts). **23/30 marks**

**Scored 42/50   84% = grade A**

# Question 3
# Men and women in the labour market

**Total for this question: 50 marks**

Study **Extracts A** and **B**, and answer **all** parts of the question that follows.

**Extract A: *Male and female labour market participation in the UK, 1968–98***

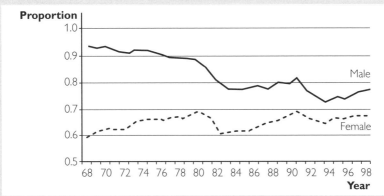

Note: The graph shows the proportion of men and women below retirement age who are in employment or self-employment.

Source: IFS briefing note no. 19, 'Inequality and living standards in Great Britain: some facts', December 2002.

**Extract B: *Explaining changes in the UK income distribution***

Two important trends have emerged in labour market participation in recent years. First, women's labour market participation has increased: women now make up 45% of the employed workforce, compared with less than 40% at the start of the 1970s. Second, there has been a sharp decline in labour market participation among men. After the recessions at the beginning of the 1980s and the 1990s, the male participa-   5
tion rate failed to return to its pre-recession level.

Some commentators have suggested that these two trends have had an important impact on the distribution of income, since they have led to an increasing polarisation between households that are 'work-rich' and 'work-poor'. This polar-
isation has occurred because of two important aspects of the changes:   10
- Increased female participation has mostly been by married women whose husbands are also in work.
- Falling male participation has mostly been in households where there were no other workers.

# data-response question 3

**Wage inequality** 15

There have also been very important changes in the hourly wages that different workers command. The male and female distributions show distinct trends. Some of the important points to note are:

- During the 1980s and 1990s the wages of the lowest-paid male workers barely grew at all in real terms, in contrast to the substantial earnings growth seen in the 20 middle and at the top of the earnings scale.
- But unlike the male wage distribution, the wages of the lowest-paid women continued to grow during this time.
- The gap between men's and women's wages has narrowed but still remains signifi- cant. The women with the highest wages tend to be those who live in households 25 with partners also commanding high wages.

**Demographic factors**

An increase in the number of less traditional family types, particularly one-adult households, both with and without children, has been matched by a decline in the number of people living in so-called traditional families. Three main trends in family 30 formation and dissolution, which are roughly common in all western societies, have been cited:

- The age at which men and women first enter marriage has increased.
- Women give birth later and have fewer children.
- Families are more subject to dissolution through divorce. 35

Source: adapted from IFS briefing note no. 19, 'Inequality and living standards in Great Britain: some facts', December 2002.

**(a)** Compare the changes, shown in Extracts A and B, in male and female participation in the UK labour market that occurred between 1968 and 1998. (4 marks)

**(b)** Lines 2–4 of Extract B state: 'Women's labour market participation has increased: …there has been a sharp decline in labour market participation among men.' Explain one reason for each of these two changes in labour market participation rates. (6 marks)

**(c)** Analyse how the changing nature of the family outlined in Extract B may have affected the distribution of income between rich and poor families in the UK. (10 marks)

**(d)** The data state that on average women are paid significantly less than men. Evaluate various economic factors that might explain differences in male and female pay. (30 marks)

■ ■ ■

## Candidate's answer

**(a)** Extract A shows that the proportion of women below retirement age in employment or self-employment rose from 60% in 1968 to just under 70% 30 years later in 1998. This rising female labour market participation was matched by a decline in male participation from about 94% in 1968 to about 78% in 1998. These are general trends over the 30-year period. Extract A also shows that participation of both men and women fell in the recessions of the early 1980s and early 1990s, as *both* men and women became unemployed. Extract B states that women now make up to 45% of the employed labour force, compared with less than 40% at the start of the 1970s.

> ✍ This is an excellent answer which, by drawing on both extracts as instructed, earns full marks. The candidate makes a clear comparison and resists the temptation to drift irrelevantly into *explaining the causes* of the changes being compared.
>
> **4/4 marks**

**(b)** This question is asking me to explain the comparison I have made in my first answer. An explanation for declining male participation lies in the *deindustrialisation process*. Deindustrialisation is the relative, and sometimes absolute, decline of manufacturing industries such as the steel industry and shipbuilding, together with primary industries such as coal mining and fishing. These industries mostly employ men, so when they go into absolute decline because they cannot compete internationally, male workers lose their jobs. This ties in with the reason for growing female participation. Growing industries in the UK have mostly been service sector industries. The skills they require, such as computer keyboard typing, suit women. Men can do this type of work, but the type of labour laid off by declining heavy manufacturing industries has found it difficult to move into the new service sector jobs that have been created.

> ✍ This is another excellent answer. The candidate has provided a good explanation for both growing female labour market participation and falling male labour market participation.
>
> **6/6 marks**

**(c)** First, the age at which men and women first marry has increased. This allows *both* men and women to continue their education and develop careers, which in most cases means that both marriage partners have well-paid jobs when they marry. Also, by saving before they marry, such people accumulate wealth that can generate investment income during the rest of the marriage partners' lives.

Second, the age at which women have children has increased, and women then give birth to fewer children. Many women can stay in full-time education longer and then train for better-paid careers. The number of better-paid double-income families has grown. And because women become better established in worthwhile careers, they can take a break for a few years to have children and then rejoin their old career, albeit often at a lower salary than male colleagues whose careers have not been interrupted. But better-paid women can usually afford to employ child-minders (giving employment usually to other more lowly paid women), thereby progressing without interruption in their highly paid careers. Having fewer children aids this trend.

However, another point mentioned in Extract B works to some extent in the opposite direction, leading to more women on low incomes. Unskilled and poorly

# data-response question 3

educated single women with children (who often give birth in their teens) may never enter the labour market. They become part of the *dependency culture*, in a sense *married to the state*, living off benefits throughout their lives.

🖉 This answer reaches the highest Level 3 mark band for part (c) of a data-response question, but does not quite earn full marks. It is strong on *explanation*, but not so strong on *analysis*. (Analysis usually involves using *theory*, such as supply and demand theory in the labour market, to develop the explanation(s) offered.)

**9/10 marks**

**(d)** There are two main reasons why women often earn less than men. First, women work predominantly in low-paid industries and occupations. Second, within many occupational groups, women are paid less than men. This is often because women are under-represented in the higher-paid posts within an occupation, rather than because women are paid less for doing the same job.

Discrimination against women in labour markets may, of course, contribute to both these sets of circumstances. In addition, women are disproportionately represented in industries where the average size of firm is small. These industries tend to pay lower wages and offer fewer promotional prospects than large firms and large industries.

Also, these industries are seldom unionised. Indeed, within all industries, women workers have been less unionised than men. This relates to another reason why women earn less than men; on average their attachment to the labour force is weaker. Each year of work experience raises the pay of both men and women by an average 3%. Yet when women leave the labour force, usually to look after young children, their potential pay falls by 3% for each year involved. If, for example, a man and woman enter employment with equal potential and after 8 years the woman leaves the workforce for a further 8 years in order to raise a family, she may re-enter the labour force 16 years in pay terms behind the man — as if she is starting work 16 years after the man.

The higher labour turnover of women also imposes costs on the employer — for example, the costs of training replacement workers. This may reduce the incentive for employers to train female workers. Similarly, women may have less incentive to spend time and money on their own education and training if they expect the benefits they will eventually receive will be less than the costs initially incurred.

'Glass ceilings' may also contribute to women often earning less than men for doing similar jobs with similar skills and qualifications. A 'glass ceiling' means that women are not promoted, despite their abilities, because of gender discrimination in the labour market. There is no doubt that significant gender discrimination does occur, in some occupations more than in others.

🖉 This is a very good answer, nearly reaching level 5 (25 to 30 marks). To reach level 5, she needs more analysis and evaluation. For analysis, she might use a supply and demand diagram to show how pay is often higher in unionised occupations, where more men than women are employed. She could also introduce the theory of wage discrimination. Many female workers, perhaps because of their social and cultural circumstances, regard themselves as second income earners within the family. Because of this, they may be prepared to work for lower pay than their husbands or partners. According to the theory of wage discrimination, workers who are willing to work for less are paid less.

While her arguments are good and sufficiently comprehensive, she includes little evaluation of the significance of the arguments. She could do this in a concluding paragraph, or by evaluating the significance of each of her explanations of the gender pay gap as she makes the point.

**24/30 marks**

**Scored 43/50  86% = grade A**

**d**ata-response question 4

# Question 4

## Social security benefits and poverty in the UK

**Total for this question: 50 marks**

Study **Extracts A, B** and **C**, and answer **all** parts of the question that follows.

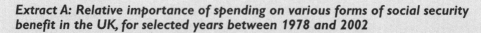

*Extract A: Relative importance of spending on various forms of social security benefit in the UK, for selected years between 1978 and 2002*

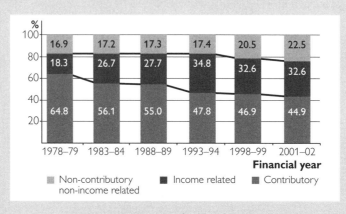

Source: Institute for Fiscal Studies, October 2000.

*Extract B: Social security benefits in the UK*

In 1999/2000, over £100 billion was spent on social security benefits in the UK. This amounts to just under £1,700 for every man, woman and child in the country, and represents 30% of total government expenditure (10.7% of GDP).

Spending on social security benefits increased almost continuously as a share of national income from 1948 to the early 1980s. It was just 4% of GDP in 1948/49, climbing over the next decades to reach a peak of 11.5% in 1983/84. During these decades, spending on social security increased for two main reasons. First, governments increased the real value or generosity of benefits. Second, the number of people eligible to claim benefits increased, especially when completely new benefits were introduced. The state old age pension provides a good example of both of these explanations. It increased in generosity from about 14% of average male earnings in 1948/49 to nearly 20% in the early 1980s. Over the same period, the number of people over the retirement age increased from 6.8 million in 1951 to 10 million in 1981.

5

10

In the early 1980s an important change was made to the way many benefits, including state pensions and unemployment benefits, are calculated. These benefits 15 are index-linked, which means that each year their nominal value rises in line with changes in an economic index. In the early 1980s, this was changed from the index of average earnings to the retail price index (RPI). This change means that old people relying on the state pension and the unemployed no longer share in increases in national prosperity. 20

Source: adapted from IFS, *A Survey of the UK Benefit System*, October 2000, available on the IFS website.

### Extract C: Means-tested benefits and the poverty trap

Over 30 million people in the UK receive income from at least one social security benefit. For contributory benefits, such as incapacity benefit, eligibility for payment depends on the claimant having made sufficient national insurance contributions (NICs). For means-tested benefits, such as income support, receipt of the benefit depends on the claimant's income and personal characteristics, such as age and family 5 type. By contrast, universal benefits such as child benefit are neither contributory nor means-tested. Universal benefits are available to all people who meet some qualification criteria, such as being parents or guardians of children.

In Britain, when your income is below a certain level — which depends on your family circumstances — you are usually eligible for means-tested benefits. When your 10 income rises you start to lose those benefits. You can think of this benefit withdrawal as a form of income tax: for each rise in income, you lose a certain amount of benefit.

Continuing high rates of benefit withdrawal constitute what has become known as the poverty trap. Working families at the low end of the income distribution, caught in the poverty trap, face the highest effective marginal tax rates in the UK. 15

Source: adapted from Maureen Mackintosh, *Redistribution*, published by the Open University Press, 1995.

(a) Using the data in Extracts A and B, describe the main changes that have occurred in the UK in spending on different forms of social security benefit. (4 marks)
(b) Extract B states that because of the way welfare benefits are now index-linked, old people and the unemployed no longer share in increases in national prosperity. Explain why. (6 marks)
(c) Analyse how means-tested benefits and universal benefits, such as child benefit mentioned in Extract C, may affect incentives to supply labour. (10 marks)
(d) Evaluate two ways of reforming the UK tax and benefits system to reduce or eliminate the poverty trap described in Extract C. (30 marks)

■ ■ ■

# data-response question 4

## Candidate's answer

**(a)** According to Extract B, spending on social security benefits rose from about 4% of GDP in 1948/49, to peak at 11.5% in 1983/84, before falling slightly to 10.7% in 1999/2000. Over the rather different period (1978–2002) shown in Extract A, non-contributory non-income related benefits and income-related benefits grew in proportionate importance (from 16.9% and 18.3% to 22.5% and 32.6% respectively). Of course, if two of the three categories of benefit rose in proportionate importance, the third category (contributory benefits) must have fallen as a percentage — from 64.8% to 44.9%.

> This is an excellent answer, which obeys the instruction to use data from both Extract A and Extract B, and to describe, rather than to explain the causes of, the main changes. The candidate clearly appreciates the fact that the data periods in Extracts A and B are not identical. He also understands that percentages add to 100%, so if one item increases in proportionate importance, one or more other items must fall in proportionate importance.
>
> **4/4 marks**

**(b)** As Extract B states, welfare benefits, such as unemployment benefit and the state old age pension, used to be index-linked to the index of average earnings. This meant that the real value of benefits rose by the same percentage each year in line with the increased value of average wages and salaries of people in work. Benefit recipients shared in increasing national prosperity. However, the change in the early 1980s to the way benefits are index-linked (linking benefit increases to the rate of inflation, as measured by the retail price index) means that the *nominal* value of benefits now rises in line with inflation, but their *real* value or purchasing power remains unchanged.

> This is a good answer as far as it goes, but it does not go quite far enough to gain all 6 marks. To earn the extra mark, the candidate needed to explain that if the real value of benefits remains unchanged, their value *relative* to average earnings falls (because the real value of the latter increases). **5/6 marks**

**(c)** Incentives in the labour market to supply labour are affected through the impact of means testing on the effective marginal rate of income tax. Because of means testing, over certain income ranges, the marginal rate of income tax is higher than 100%. When this is the case, disposable income actually falls following an increase in pre-tax income. This must have a disincentive effect on workers. Why work longer hours if disposable income falls as a result? By contrast, universal benefits do not affect the marginal rate of income tax, so they do not have a disincentive effect.

> While the candidate clearly understands the difference between means-tested and universal benefits, his answer is short of *analysis*. He needs to analyse how the marginal tax rate affects the supply of labour. An increase in income tax is equivalent to a cut in the hourly wage rate. If a worker's supply curve of labour slopes

upwards to the right (as illustrated in Figure 21(a) on page 52), the worker responds to the wage rate cut by supplying fewer hours of labour. Means testing away a worker's ability to claim benefit as income rises increases the effective marginal tax rate and reduces the effective marginal wage rate. This in turn reduces the incentive to supply labour. But if a worker's supply curve of labour is backward bending, as in Figure 21(b), the worker might respond to the cut in the effective wage rate by working longer hours. Either way, disaffected workers may respond to loss of benefit by deciding to supply labour in the informal 'underground' economy, sometimes called the black economy.

**5/10 marks**

**(d)** The two methods of reforming the UK tax and benefits system to reduce or eliminate the poverty trap, which I shall evaluate, are (i) integrating the benefits system into the tax system; and (ii) significantly increasing the level of income at which people start paying income tax.

**(i)** *Integrating the benefits system into the tax system.* The poverty trap (or earnings trap, to give it a more accurate name) occurs in the zone of overlap between the income tax threshold and the means-tested benefit ceiling. Consider what happens if a worker whose earnings fall in this range receives a pay rise. The worker pays more income tax, but also loses the ability to claim benefits, part of which is means-tested away. If the income tax system and the benefit system were integrated, the income tax threshold (which is the level of income at which income tax starts to be paid) and the benefit ceiling (which is the level of income beyond which means-tested benefits cannot be claimed) could be set at the same level. The zone of overlap would disappear, and with it the poverty trap!

**(ii)** *Significantly increasing the level of income at which people start paying income tax.* Fifty years ago, workers on average wages in the UK paid no income tax because their incomes were below the income tax threshold. Over the next 50 years, two factors caused most low-paid workers to move across the tax threshold, with many of them also entering the poverty trap. The first factor was rising nominal and real incomes, making most people better off. The second factor was 'fiscal drag'. Fiscal drag occurs when each year, personal tax allowances (and resulting tax thresholds) are raised by less than inflation. This reduces the real value of personal tax allowances and causes the tax threshold to move down the income pyramid. In turn, this drags the low-paid, who previously paid no income tax, into the 'tax net'. Raising personal tax allowances by more than the rate of inflation reverses this process, and 'claws back' fiscal drag that has taken place in previous years. It removes the low-paid from the income tax net, and hence reduces or eliminates the poverty trap. This reform could, of course, be used in conjunction with my first suggested reform, integrating the benefits system into the tax system.

Just as in his answer to part (c) the candidate did not sufficiently obey the key instruction to *analyse*, so this answer is short of *evaluation*. (Remember, analysis and evaluation are the skills mainly tested by the last part of data-response and essay

# data-response question 4

questions.) Again, he shows plenty of relevant knowledge, but he needs to develop his answer further. He could do this by discussing the disadvantages of his proposed reforms, and then assessing whether the advantages exceed the disadvantages. For example, merging the benefit and tax systems might lead to benefits being assessed and dispensed by the Inland Revenue. It can be argued that the taxman is not the most appropriate authority to deal with benefits whose main purpose is to reduce poverty. People without a tax code may end up without benefits and living in needless poverty. Also, some benefits are targeted at child poverty. These benefits are more likely to reach the children for whom they are intended if paid in cash to the mother rather than through an adjustment to the father's tax code. While it is unlikely that many candidates would consider arguments like these, there is a basic point all candidates should be capable of making. Raising tax thresholds to remove the low-waged from the tax net is likely to reduce the government's total tax revenue. This implies either a cut in spending on public services or increases in other taxes, such as VAT, to make up the lost revenue. **20/30 marks**

**Scored 34/50  68% = grade A/B borderline**

# Essay questions

## Question 1

## Objectives and growth of firms

**(a)** With the use of an appropriate diagram, explain how a firm maximises profit, and briefly describe two other objectives a firm may have. (20 marks)

**(b)** Identify and evaluate possible benefits and costs that might result from a firm's growth through takeover or merger. (30 marks)

■ ■ ■

### Candidate's answer

**(a)** The diagram I have drawn below shows a firm maximising profit. Profit is the difference between total revenue (TR) and total cost (TC). At low levels of output, the firm would make a loss because to start with total costs are greater than total sales revenue. This is because the firm still has to pay fixed costs even when output and sales are zero and no revenue is being earned. The firm breaks even (i.e. makes zero profit or loss) at the level of output at which the TR curve crosses the TC curve. Profits are made at levels of output above this point. Maximum profits are made at $Q_1$ where the TR and TC curves are furthest apart. Profits are shown by the vertical distance AB.

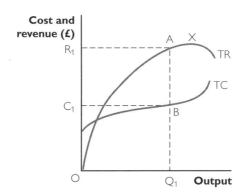

The assumption that firms aim to maximise profit is a simplification made by economists in order to analyse the theory of the firm. In the real world, firms may have other objectives. For some firms, revenue maximisation is more important than profit maximisation. On my diagram above, revenue maximisation is shown at point X. Beyond this point, the TR curve begins to fall and marginal revenue (MR) becomes negative.

For my second alternative objective, I shall introduce the concept of *satisficing*. Whereas *maximising* theories of the firm (such as the profit and revenue-maximising theories I have mentioned) are a part of 'orthodox' or 'traditional' economic theory, some economists (who are known as *organisationalists* or *behaviourists*) have adopted a different approach. These economists model firms as *satisficers* rather than as *maximisers*. Because a firm's managers are unable to locate a marginalist point such as MR = MC, in practice they set minimum acceptable levels of achievement. They satisfice rather than maximise. Minimum targets will be set for such variables as sales revenue, profit, growth, stockholding of raw materials and so on.

'Organisationalists' see the firm as an organisation comprising coalitions of different groups within the firm, such as production managers, financial managers, production workers, research scientists, etc., each possessing a different group objective or objectives. A coalition within an organisation is any group sharing a consensus on the goals it should pursue. Managers may form one coalition seeking prestige, power and high salaries, while other coalitions would include production workers wanting higher wages and improved job security and working conditions, and shareholders desiring higher profits. Differing goals or aspirations will result in group conflict. A firm's top managers ultimately make key decisions to resolve conflict between the different interest groups within the organisation. In order to satisfy the aspirations of as many groups within the organisation as possible, this inevitably involves compromise and the setting of minimum rather than maximum targets. Hence the concept of satisficing to replace maximising, to describe how decisions are made within complex organisations.

🖉 This is an excellent answer that earns full marks. It is an unusual answer in two respects. First, the candidate explains and illustrates profit maximisation using total revenue and cost curves rather than marginal and average cost and revenue curves. Second, the candidate displays far more knowledge about satisficing (as an alternative assumption to maximising) than is actually needed to earn full marks.

With respect to the first point, although the candidate does not mention it, he has drawn a diagram to show a monopoly or imperfectly competitive firm maximising profit. The evidence for this is the TR curve. In monopoly, total revenue rises as output and sales increase, but rises at a slower rate than sales. This is because a monopolist can only sell more by reducing the good's price. As the candidate quite rightly states, marginal revenue will eventually become negative. Beyond this point, which is the sales revenue-maximising level of output, the TR curve falls. In perfect competition, by contrast, TR is shown by a straight line from origin.

**20/20 marks**

**(b)** A benefit of external growth through takeover or merger is speed. External growth allows a firm to acquire quickly the already up-and-running assets of another company, without having to build them up from scratch, as is the case in the much slower process of internal or organic growth. These assets could include: the knowledge, skills and expertise of its managers and workforce; any inventions, patents and other intellectual property the acquired business owns; land and property in the form of buildings and plant; and any cash on deposit in bank accounts owned by the acquired business.

The last two points I have just mentioned are likely to be significant if *asset stripping* is a main motive for launching a takeover bid. Asset stripping occurs when the acquiring company judges that its victim's profits are smaller than they could be, largely because the victim owns hidden assets that are not delivering as much profit as they would in an alternative use. This means that the victim company can be bought on the cheap, at or near its relatively low share price, which results from the poor management performance of the company's current owners. Once acquired, the new owner closes the company down, sacks the workers and gets his hands on the victim's hidden assets, usually land — which can be sold or converted to an alternative use — or a 'cash mountain' that the previous owners were not using productively.

Vertical growth backwards by purchasing a previously independent company supplying components allows a business to benefit from better control over its supply chain, for example by ensuring quality and specification of components. Likewise the acquisition of retail outlets in the distribution chain (vertical growth forwards) achieves better control over market conditions in which the firm's products are sold.

Acquiring firms producing similar goods (horizontal external growth) enables a company to achieve quickly greater *scale*. The larger firm benefits from economies of scale. Horizontal mergers are especially attractive when two companies have complementary product ranges, for example a car company specialising in large executive cars acquiring a car company whose main business is smaller family cars. As another example, a supermarket company that is strong in the south of England may merge with a similar company whose stores are in the north and Scotland. Finally, the purchase of a company in a completely different line of business (a lateral takeover) allows the acquiring company to gain the benefits of diversification — that is, not having 'all its eggs in one basket'. However, lateral takeovers also have disadvantages. The acquiring company may lack management expertise in the industries and markets into which it is diversifying, and end up with higher unit costs resulting from managerial diseconomies of scale. This explains why many highly diversified businesses which were the product of 'merger mania' in the 1980s have, in more recent years, been broken up. Recent and current fashion has been to 'demerge' — that is, to sell off — often through management buyouts, peripheral or 'non-core' parts of over-diversified conglomerates, and to concentrate on the core activities of the slimmed-down rump of the previously much larger business.

✍ While the candidate displays considerable knowledge and understanding of external growth and related concepts, unfortunately the answer has some significant weaknesses. The question instructs the candidate to 'Identify and evaluate possible benefits and costs'. He identifies a number of benefits (for the firm taking over or merging with other firms), but he writes much less about possible costs or disadvantages of external growth. Second, his answer lacks explicit evaluation of benefits and costs. With a question like this, the skill of evaluation is best shown in a conclusion which argues that the benefits exceed the costs, or vice versa, or that it all depends on circumstances and each case must be judged on its merits. To reach Levels 4 and 5, evaluation is required. Because this answer contains explanation and a little analysis, but no evaluation, it reaches Level 3 (11–17 marks), but a higher mark cannot be awarded.

Evaluation can also be displayed by discussing: benefits and costs for whom? Benefits (and costs) for a takeover raider or corporate raider may not be benefits (and costs) for the company being acquired. Nor may they necessarily be benefits (and costs) for the wider community. Takeovers or mergers that are in the private interest of the shareholders or owners of the companies involved are not necessarily in the public interest or social interest. A main function of the government's competition policy (see 'Industrial policy' p. 40) is to investigate contentious takeovers and mergers to decide if there may be a possible conflict between private and social costs and benefits.

The candidate explains some of the motives for acquisitions, but without evaluating their benefits and costs. The asset-stripping motive is a good example. According to its critics, asset stripping is the 'unacceptable face of capitalism', in which the 'making of money' replaces the 'making of things'. Firms producing useful goods and services that meet economic needs and increase economic welfare are closed down, with the raider stripping the victim of cash and land — the latter often being used for property speculation. Not so, say other economists. Asset stripping is simply part of the necessary restructuring of markets and industries which takes place through new owners acquiring under-performing companies and converting their assets to more profitable and productive uses. A Level 5 answer would explain both sides of this issue before concluding whether an asset-stripping takeover is good or bad for the public interest as well as for the owners of the acquiring and the acquired companies. **17/30 marks**

**Scored 37/50    74% = grade B**

# Question 2
## Perfect competition

'Because perfect competition does not exist in the real world, the model of perfect competition has no economic use.'

**(a)** Explain how price and output are determined in perfect competition, both for the whole market and for a particular firm within the market. (20 marks)

**(b)** Do you agree that the model of perfect competition is of little or no economic use? Justify your answer. (30 marks)

■ ■ ■

## Candidate's answer

**(a)** Perfect competition is defined by the following characteristics:

    (i) a very large number of buyers (consumers) and sellers (firms);

    (ii) each with perfect information about the market;

    (iii) each buyer and seller can buy or sell as much as it wants at the ruling market price;

    (iv) but cannot through individual action influence the ruling market price;

    (v) a uniform or homogeneous product;

    (vi) no barriers to entry into or exit from the market in the long run.

The fourth condition I have listed means that each firm is a passive price-taker. Short-run equilibrium is shown in the diagrams below.

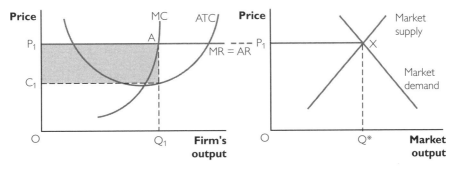

Equilibrium price ($P_1$) and output ($Q^*$) in the market as a whole are determined at point X, where market demand equals market supply. For each firm in the market, $P_1$ is both average revenue (AR) and marginal revenue (MR). The firm's profit-maximising level of output is $Q_1$, immediately below point A, which determines the level of output at which MR = MC. Because the price line at $P_1$ is above the firm's average total cost (ATC) curve, in short-run equilibrium the firm makes supernormal profit, which is shown by the shaded rectangle in the left-hand panel of the diagram.

In the short run, perfectly competitive firms make supernormal profit. However, in the long run, when there are no barriers to market entry, any supernormal profit made by incumbent firms (that is, firms already in the market) encourages new firms to enter the market. As the next pair of diagrams show, the entry of new firms causes the market supply curve to shift rightward from $S_1$ to $S_2$, which in turn causes the ruling market price to fall to P*. Market equilibrium is determined at point Y. Market output has increased to Q**, but this is now produced by a larger number of firms (the original incumbent firms, plus the new entrants). For each firm, the fall in price eliminates the supernormal profit that the firm had previously made at the higher price $P_1$. Each firm, producing output $Q_2$ (immediately below point B where MR = MC), now makes only normal profit. This is the long-run or true equilibrium position both for the whole market and for each firm within the market.

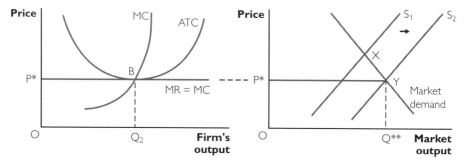

☑ Although the candidate begins his answer with a list of the conditions of perfect competition, he resists the temptation to drift into 'write all you know about perfect competition' mode. Instead, his answer remains completely focused on the question. He writes everything required by the question and so earns full marks.

**20/20 marks**

**(b)** Because the six conditions or characteristics that I listed at the start of my answer to part (a) are so demanding, no market actually displays all these characteristics at the same time. Some markets, such as agricultural markets, approximate to perfect competition. So, if no real-world market is perfectly competitive, can the theory of perfect competition be of any possible use?

Critics of free-market economic theory argue that, because it is unreal and an artificial abstraction, perfect competition only has an ideological use. They believe that perfect competition is ideologically loaded to favour the free-market view of how the economy should operate.

By contrast, free-market economists justify the usefulness of perfect competition in the following way. They start from the uncontentious point, agreed by all economists, that economic theory is based on developing economic models which describe particular aspects of economic behaviour. Perfect competition is an example of an economic model. The ultimate purpose of a model is to derive predictions about economic behaviour. A 'good' model makes predictions that stand up to empirical testing (that is, their predictions are consistent with the evidence). Free-market economists believe that, despite the lack of realism of its assumptions, perfect competition is a 'good' economic model because of its predictive and explanatory power. For example, the theory of perfect competition predicts that, if firms incur unnecessarily high costs or produce goods that consumers do not want, the firms must mend their ways or go bust. Providing real-world markets approximate to perfect competition, Adam Smith's hidden or invisible hand of the market will discipline firms that stray away from the cost-reducing path predicted by the model of perfect competition.

My own view is that, to some extent, perfect competition is a useful model for the reasons just mentioned, but I agree with the model's critics that it models a make-believe world. Indeed, it is interesting to speculate on the forms competition might take in a perfectly competitive market economy. The first point to note is that price competition, in the form of 'price wars' or price cutting by individual firms, would not take place. In perfect competition all firms are passive 'price-takers', able to sell whatever output they produce at the ruling market price determined in the market as a whole. Firms could not possibly gain sales or market share by price cutting. Other forms of competition, involving the use of advertising, packaging, brand imaging or the provision of after-sales service to differentiate the firm's product from those of other firms, would simply destroy the conditions of perfect competition. These are examples of precisely the forms of competition which are prevalent, together with price competition, in the imperfectly competitive markets of the real economy in which we live. So the only form of competition both available to firms and also compatible with maintaining the conditions of perfect competition would be 'cost-cutting' competition in order to make supernormal profits. But the existence of 'cost-cutting' competition in a perfect market can also be questioned. Why should firms finance research into cost-cutting technical progress when they know that other firms have instant access to all market information and that any above-normal profits resulting from successful cost cutting can only be temporary? It is useful also to consider the nature of competition in a perfect market from the perspective of a typical consumer. The choice facing a consumer would be simul-taneously very broad yet very narrow. The consumer would have the doubtful luxury of maximum choice in terms of the number of firms or suppliers from whom to purchase a product, yet each firm would be supplying a completely identical good or service at exactly the same price! In this sense, the range of choice in a perfectly competitive world would be extremely narrow.

The introduction to the specification for Module 5 includes the following advice: 'This module...will require candidates to use and evaluate more complex micro-economic models, for example perfect competition...and to develop further their critical approach to such economic models and methods of enquiry.' This candidate clearly understands the purpose of economic model building. **30/30 marks**

**Scored 50/50    100% = grade A**

# Question 3
# Monopoly and economic efficiency

'Monopoly is statically inefficient but dynamically efficient.'
(a) Explain this statement. (20 marks)
(b) Evaluate the view that the existence of monopoly can be justified, providing
    the market is contestable. (30 marks)

■ ■ ■

## Candidate's answer

(a) A firm is statically efficient only when it produces at the lowest point on its average
   total cost (ATC) curve. Points of static efficiency are shown at A and B on the two
   short-run average cost (SRATC) curves in my diagram.

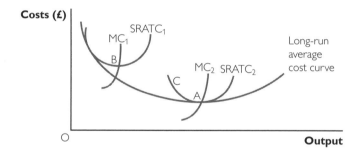

Dynamic efficiency, by contrast, results from improvements in static efficiency that
take place over time. The development of a new process for manufacturing a good,
which reduces average costs of production, is an example of dynamic efficiency.
In my diagram, the movement from SRATC$_1$ to SRATC$_2$ represents an improvement
in dynamic efficiency, resulting from the firm's ability to benefit from economies
of scale, which enables the firm to move to a lower short-run average cost curve.
   Providing the market is large enough, a monopoly can benefit from economies
of scale. It can produce on SRATC$_2$, whereas smaller competitive firms might be
constrained to producing on SRATC$_1$. A monopoly is thus likely to be dynamically
efficient. It could also be statically efficient on SRATC$_2$, but only if it produces at
point A on this curve. However, because monopolies often restrict output, in order
to raise the price they can charge and make supernormal profit, the monopoly
may in fact end up producing at point C. This point is statically inefficient. My
analysis has shown, therefore, that a monopoly can be dynamically efficient but
statically inefficient.

🖉 This is an excellent answer, as far as it goes, but it does not go quite far enough.
   With one exception, what the candidate has written is relevant and accurate.

However, the answer defines static efficiency solely in terms of productive efficiency (though this term is not mentioned explicitly). The Module 5 specification requires knowledge, understanding and application of two static efficiency concepts: productive efficiency and allocative efficiency. The candidate needs to develop her point about a monopoly restricting output and raising price. She should explain that this is allocatively inefficient, as P > MC. **15/20 marks**

**(b)** Compared to perfect competition, a monopoly has the incentive to innovate (because the firm can enjoy the fruits of successful innovation in the form of monopoly profit), and by growing in size, it can achieve economies of scale and reduce costs.

In recent years, the theory of contestable markets has also been used to justify monopoly. A market is contestable when a new firm can enter the market without being deterred by entry barriers, and without incurring sunk costs that are irrecoverable, should the firm decide to leave the market.

To develop my answer further, I shall use the recent federal court case in America, in which the US Justice Department prosecuted Microsoft, with a view to getting the court to break up Microsoft into a number of smaller firms, so as to reduce its alleged monopoly position in the PC software market. Economists hired by Microsoft argued that, although it is a monopoly in the sense that the company has over 90% of the PC operating system market, Microsoft has no monopoly power because the market is contestable. They argued: (i) if Microsoft acted as a profit-maximising monopolist, it would charge a price of over $100 for its Windows operating system; (ii) because of an absence of entry barriers, other firms would then enter the market and undercut Microsoft's price; (iii) to prevent this happening, Microsoft actually charges a price (around $35) that is much lower than the profit-maximising price. This means that Microsoft sets *limit prices* for its products. Microsoft argues that consumers benefit from its limit pricing policy. Conversely, consumers would suffer greatly (from higher prices and less technical innovation and new products) if the US courts ever decided to force Microsoft to split into smaller firms.

My conclusion is, if a monopoly behaves 'virtuously' and does not abuse its monopoly power, and if the market is sufficiently contestable, its dominant position can be justified — but only as long as the firm continues to behave itself. To try to ensure this outcome, the monopoly must be policed by a regulatory agency set up by the government. Even then, however, there is always the danger that the agency, lacking sufficient technical knowledge of the firm(s) it is regulating, will be ineffective and/or subject to regulatory capture.

The candidate again writes an excellent answer, which displays a depth and breadth of relevant knowledge. I particularly like her use of the Microsoft court case to provide evidence for the arguments she makes. The answer reaches Level 5 (25–30 marks). **26/30 marks**

**Scored 41/50   82% = grade A**

# Question 4
# Market failure and government failure

(a) **Explain how free provision of a merit good, such as health care or education, may lead to problems of government failure replacing those of market failure.** (20 marks)

(b) **Assess the case for creating a market in tradable permits to pollute as a method of correcting the market failure resulting from the discharge of pollution into the atmosphere.** (30 marks)

■ ■ ■

## Candidate's answer

**(a)** Market failure occurs whenever markets perform badly or fail to function at all. Government failure occurs when government intervention in markets, often intended to correct a market failure, is ineffective and the market failure persists, or — more seriously — the intervention creates a completely new problem which is worse than the market failure the intervention was intended to correct.

A merit good can be defined as a good such as education or health care, for which the social benefits of consumption (received by the whole community) exceed the private benefits enjoyed by the individual consumer. The explanation for this stems from the fact that when an individual benefits from education or health care, he or she generates positive externalities which benefit the whole community. Everybody benefits from an individual being healthy, if only because there is one less person from whom to catch a disease!

Markets can provide merit goods, as the existence of private education and health care shows, but arguably they under-provide them. The socially optimal level of consumption of a merit good occurs when the marginal social benefit of consumption equals the marginal social cost of consumption (MSB = MSC). But when people have to pay market prices for merit goods, markets can only provide up to the point at which MPB = MPC. Because positive externalities are generated, this is below the socially optimal level of provision and consumption.

To encourage consumption, governments often provide merit goods 'free' — that is, at zero price to the consumer — financing provision out of general taxation. The case for such free provision is reinforced by the *equity* reason for the government providing merit goods. Arguably, if market prices are charged for the provision of merit goods, the poor cannot afford to pay and end up going without.

But free provision can lead to government failure. Consumers tend to undervalue goods and services that are provided free by the state. Doctors' patients who fail to turn up for (free) appointments provide an example. Also, there is no guarantee that the planning mechanism, which, in the absence of a market, decides how much of the merit good to produce and supply, will get things right. Planners may make wasteful and inefficient use of scarce resources, and they may over-supply merit goods to some people while under-supplying to others.

Equity problems may also persist with free state provision, though in different forms than when the market supplies the merit good. 'Postcode' rationing means that people living in the right locations have access to good free state schools, while the poor often have to make do with a significantly inferior service.

> ✍ While good, this answer could be improved in two ways. First, although the candidate explains why markets under-provide merit goods, he does not include a diagram. A diagram such as Figure 20(a) on page 49 would improve his answer. Second, his explanation of possible government failure, though well focused, would benefit from a little more development. **18/20 marks**

**(b)** Many economic activities, both industrial and in the field of consumption, such as driving a car for pleasure, lead to the emission of pollution, which is a negative externality. Because motorists dump pollution on innocent 'third parties', in a market situation, motoring ends up too cheap, with motorists driving their cars too much.

Two policies used by governments to try to correct this market failure are pollution taxes, based on the 'polluter must pay' principle, and regulation. A pollution tax works 'with the market', creating incentives for the polluter to reduce emissions in order to avoid, quite legally, having to pay the tax. However, a pollution tax, on its own, is not enough; it needs to be backed up by compulsion in the form of regulation. Likewise, regulation on its own is too heavy-handed: it is a 'stick without a carrot'. Carrots are preferable to get people to alter their economic behaviour voluntarily.

This is where a market in tradable permits to pollute has advantages. Such a market is a mix of regulation and market-based incentives. The regulation takes the form of maximum emission limits that are reduced each year, say by 10%. But regulation on its own does not create incentives to over-comply — that is, to reduce pollution voluntarily by more than 10%. Tradable permits to pollute create just such an incentive. Polluters who over-comply can sell their 'spare' pollution permits to those who cannot comply — and who end up under-complying. By providing a means for polluters who reduce emissions by more than the law requires to make money from over-compliance by selling unused pollution permits, market-based incentives are created. And the under-complying purchasers of the 'spare' pollution permits also have an incentive to clean up their act, to avoid having to spend money on buying extra permits to pollute to enable them to discharge pollution over and above the maximum emission limits.

I therefore believe that a strong case exists for creating markets in permits to pollute. It would, of course, be easier to introduce such markets for polluters such as power stations. It would be difficult to see how a market in pollution permits could be created for private motorists.

# e ssay question 4

📝 The candidate shows good knowledge and understanding of markets in permits to pollute, and provides a sound argument for introducing such markets. Once again his answer would benefit from inclusion and explanation of an appropriate diagram, similar to Figure 18 on page 47. A lack of balance reduces the overall mark. Because the candidate makes little mention of possible disadvantages of markets in permits to pollute, he only picks up a couple of evaluation marks. Overall, the answer is quite strong on analysis but weak on evaluation, so I have placed it in Level 4 (18–24 marks). **19/30 marks**

**Scored 37/50    74% = grade A**

# Question 5
## Trade unions and the labour market

**(a) Why are some workers paid more than other workers?** (20 marks)

**(b) Evaluate the view that trade unions can only increase wages for their
members at the expense of reduced levels of employment.** (30 marks)

■ ■ ■

## Candidate's answer

**(a)** There are a number of reasons why some workers are paid more than other
workers. Perhaps the main reason lies in different market conditions in different
labour markets. My diagram below shows supply and demand conditions in two
different labour markets, the market for investment bankers and the market for
road sweepers. The supply and demand curves in the market for investment
bankers intersect at a much higher market-clearing wage or salary, hence their
much higher pay.

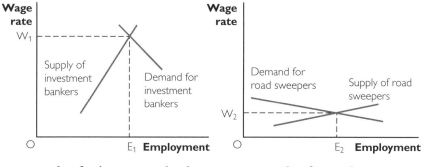

*Market for investment bankers*     *Market for road sweepers*

Another reason for different levels of pay is different degrees of competitiveness
in labour markets. In a monopsony labour market, a single employer possesses
sufficient market power to drive wages down to a level that may be much less
than in a perfectly competitive labour market.

    Different requirements for training and skill can also explain different wages.
If a long training period is required, wages tend to be higher. If few people have
the aptitude or natural talent for a particular job, again their pay tends to be high.
David Beckham is one of the highest-paid footballers in the world, both for his
talent as a player and for his celebrity status.

    Generally speaking, wages are higher in markets where (a) demand for the
product that labour produces is increasing, and (b) workers do not face competition
from third world countries where wages are much lower.

# e ssay question 5

📝 When a question similar to this was set in the first Unit 5 examination in June 2002, a disappointingly high proportion of candidates wrote superficial 'common-sense' answers, devoid of any economic theory. This candidate includes economic theory in her answer, but unfortunately she doesn't develop the theory sufficiently. She states correctly that demand and supply curves are in different positions in different labour markets, and she uses a good example, but to earn a higher mark, she needs to offer theoretical explanation of *why* the curves are in different positions. With questions like this, candidates must select relevant elements of labour market theory and then apply theory to explain the issue(s) posed by the question. **11/20 marks**

**(b)** Trade unions are monopoly suppliers of labour and, like all monopolies, they are bad because they interfere in the efficient working of competitive markets and cause market failure. This is shown by my diagram below, which illustrates how a trade union raises wages at the expense of employment.

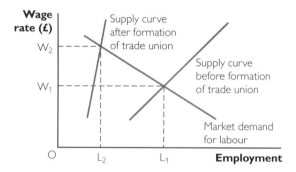

As my diagram shows, trade unions shift the supply curve of labour leftward. They may also make the supply curve less elastic. They do this by introducing labour restrictive practices into the labour market. The main restrictive practice is a 'closed shop'. A 'closed shop' prevents workers who are not members of the union from getting jobs with the employer. Unions may also call their members out on strike, or operate overtime bans and working to rule, when employers refuse to give in to their wage demands.

Trade unions are run by communists who want to smash capitalism, abolish the monarchy and bring down the government. As strikes by coal miners and firemen show, all they want to do is to hold the country to ransom. It should not be allowed. Unions should be banned and their leaders sent to prison.

📝 Despite being short and drifting into an anti-union rant, strong on opinion but devoid of economics, the diagram and accompanying explanation allow the answer to reach the Level 2/Level 3 borderline. To reach a higher mark, some analysis of how a union may be able to raise both wages and employment needs to be included. Examination questions on labour markets and unions often seem to produce this sort of answer, with the occasional appearance of an anti-capitalist rant. **10/20 marks**

**Scored 21/50   42% = grade D**